Groupwork

109

Groupwork

Third Edition

Allan Brown

arena

First published in hardback by Gower Publishing Company Limited.

First published in paperback by Ashgate Publishing 1992

This edition published 1994 by
Arena
Ashgate Publishing Limited
Gower House
Croft Road
Aldershot
Hants GU11 3HR
England

Ashgate Publishing Company
Old Post Road
Brookfield
Vermont 05036
USA

Reprinted 1995

A CIP catalogue record for this book is available from the British Library

ISBN 1 85742 087 X

Typeset in 11 point Times by Photoprint, Torquay, Devon and printed in Great Britain by Hartnolls Limited, Bodmin, Cornwall.

Contents

Acknowledgements

1st edition (1979)

I am indebted to numerous people who have shared with me their groupwork experience, feelings and ideas. They include many group members, social work students and teachers, social workers and probation officers in Britain and in Michigan, USA. In particular, Frank Maple of the University of Michigan, and Nano McCaughan, recently of the National Institute of Social Work, London, have stimulated and encouraged me in my interest in groupwork.

I would like to thank Christine Stones, Derek Lockhart, Phyllida Parsloe and Brian Caddick (of Bristol University) for reading draft chapters and offering support and critical comment.

I am grateful to Margaret Harris and Georgina Coleman for typing drafts, and to Pam Gallagher for typing the final manuscript. It is doubtful whether I could ever have completed the task without the loving support of my wife, Celia, who has given me encouragement when I most needed it.

2nd edition (1986)

I am again indebted to the many people from whom I have continued to learn about groupwork. A special thanks this time to Carol Keen for typing all the revised parts of the manuscript so helpfully and efficiently.

3rd edition (1992)

I would like to acknowledge the major contribution of my former colleague, Roger Clough, to many of the ideas in Chapter 5 which we developed together in *Groups and Groupings*.

I am indebted to Margaret Boushel, Jenny Lewis, Tara Mistry and Christine Weaver for reading a draft of Chapter 6 and offering many helpful comments for improving it.

Celia has once again been amazingly patient and supportive as I have spent numerous evenings and weekends banging away on my word processor and filling the house with the whirr of the noisy printer!

Introduction to the Third Edition

It is now thirteen years since the first edition of this book appeared, and what exciting developments there have been in groupwork in Britain, Europe and all over the world since that time! The hope I expressed in my introduction to the second edition that a specialist groupwork journal would be published in Britain/Europe before the third edition appeared has become a reality with the launch of the journal *Groupwork* in 1988. The large number of references in this edition to articles which have appeared in that journal are testimony to the contribution it has already made to the development of groupwork theory and practice. A further measure of this progress has been the launch of an annual European Groupwork Symposium in 1991. Whilst these are healthy indications of the growing independent strength of groupwork on this side of the Atlantic it is important to acknowledge our indebtedness to our friends and colleagues in North America for their inspiration and support in all these developments.

It is against this background that I have been preparing this third edition. I have been particularly conscious of the need to give much more detailed consideration to two topics not given adequate coverage in earlier editions, as well as to revising and expanding some other key sections.

The first of the two new chapters (5) addresses the issue of groupwork in day and residential centres. These are two settings where so much happens in groups of different kinds, yet the literature has barely recognised, much less actually addressed, the special features of these groups and 'groupings' (a term coined to describe the many different kinds of gathering that occur). It is essential to recognise that life and work in these group living settings require special kinds of group skills in addition to those already well established for fieldwork groups.

The second new chapter (6) is an attempt to understand the significance of race and gender in groups and groupwork practice, and to begin to develop a framework for anti-discriminatory practice. This chapter has been a considerable challenge for me, writing inescapably from the perspective of a white middle-class man. I hope that readers who have not as yet given very much thought to the issues I address will find it helpful and influential in their practice, and others, particularly those from oppressed groups, will be spurred on both to critique the level I have reached in my understanding, and to put their own perspective and understanding into writing new formulations which will take us all further forward as we seek to be genuinely anti-discriminatory in our work together in groups.

Other sections of the book which have been extended and revised include those on: group composition; open groups; aspects of co-working; and groupwork consultation.

Finally, I have updated the bibliography to include references for some of the important material that has been published in the last six years. The bibliography is now quite lengthy and should be a useful source of reference for more experienced groupworkers. To make it more manageable for those relatively new to groupwork I have asterisked (*) a range of publications which between them provide a good basis for groupwork practice and theory.

1 Groupwork in Social Work

Groupwork coming of age

Groupwork has come a long way in Britain since the 1960s when it was a relatively scarce commodity. It was rarely included in social work training courses, carried an unhelpful mystique associated with sensitivity and encounter groups, and was often regarded as an idiosyncratic activity in those agencies where it was practised by innovative social workers. The available literature was North American. In the USA at that time groupwork was already well established as a social work method, going through a phase of being separated off as a distinct specialism. This changed subsequently in the 1970s when groupwork became reintegrated with mainstream practice, and it has moved forward with a whole new vigour and impetus since 1978 when the journal *Social Work with Groups* was launched, and 1979 when the first of the North American annual groupwork symposia was held. These symposia continue to flourish as a source of inspiration and knowledge building for groupwork theoreticians and practitioners.

The 1970s saw groupwork gradually being taken more seriously in Britain, perhaps partly due to the North American influence, but more likely due to the push for diversification and improvement of practice intervention methods. This arose in part from the discouraging research evaluations of the efficacy of traditional one-to-one casework methods. A British groupwork literature began to appear at this time and a number of introductory texts were published in the period 1975–1980 (Davies, 1975; Douglas, 1976; Douglas, 1978; McCaughan, 1978; Brown, 1979; Heap, 1979) offering a firmer basis for groupwork learning during training, and for groupwork practice in agencies. There was increasing evidence from social workers (see Stevenson, Parsloe *et al.*, 1978) of a widespread wish to use groupwork methods being tempered by a lack of encouragement (if not active opposition) in some agencies. The picture in Social Se:vice Departments was patchy with some appointing specialist groupwork consultants (see Laming and Sturton, 1978; McCaughan, 1985) and others treating groupwork as a marginal activity. The one sphere in which group methods were used very extensively was in Intermediate Treatment for adolescents (Jones and Kerslake, 1979). In many Probation Areas groupwork was achieving recognition as a mainstream method of working with offenders (see Brown and Seymour, 1983), and this trend has continued as a recent national survey of the amount and range of groupwork in the probation service has confirmed (Caddick, 1991). Some voluntary agencies like the Family Service Units were already using groups as a mainstream method of working.

The growth of family centres and a whole range of day and short-term residential provision, often pioneered by voluntary agencies, offers enormous scope for working with people in groups, both formal and informal (see Chapter 5 in this book). In parallel with these developments in 'client' groups there has been a growing recognition of the importance of staff groups, with a recognition of the social work team as a group to be facilitated and developed with the same levels of care and skill (Parsloe, 1981).

Several trends can be discerned in the development of groupwork since about 1985. The first of these is an increased level of sophistication in the quality of basic skills and techniques as taught on training courses and reflected in the literature. Further basic texts have been published (see for example, Heap, 1985; Whitaker, 1985; Houston, 1984 and 1990a edn; Brown, A., 1986 edn; Benson, 1987; Preston-Shoot, 1987) and a number of training manuals are in use (see for example, Ball and Sowa, 1985; Kemp and Taylor, 1990; Henderson and Foster, 1991). The publication since 1988 of a UK-based journal, *Groupwork*, has provided a medium for the dissemination of practice and conceptual developments, and many of the articles which have appeared in that journal are referenced elsewhere in this book.

A second trend is a shift from 'generic' groupwork to the specific knowledge and skills needed for working with particular user groups and issues, and in particular ways. Five recent publications reflect this trend. Brown and Clough (1989) have edited a book which articulates the experience of practitioners in day and residential settings as they have evolved group approaches suited to group living contexts, an area previously largely neglected in the literature. The *Groupwork* journal (Kerslake and Brown, 1990) has carried a special issue on groupwork in the sphere of child sexual abuse, where group methods, whether with abused children, adult survivors or perpetrators, are often the method of choice. Another special issue, on groupwork with offenders (Brown and Caddick, 1991) gives some indication both of the range of groups being used and the values questions being raised about the compatibility of empowerment and control in a criminal justice setting. The fourth publication is the full articulation by Mullender and Ward (1991) of the self-directed model of groupwork, an approach predicated on specific principles of empowerment and a facilitator role for the worker. The fifth is the first book in the UK specifically on a feminist groupwork perspective, by Butler and Wintram (1991).

The third trend is that illustrated by the last two publications, namely a deep concern about inequalities and social discrimination being replicated in groups. The response is recognising the need to develop practice principles and methods which provide positive action both for equality of opportunity in in-group experience, and positive action through groups to confront discrimination in the wider communities and groupings to which group members and others belong. One of the tasks for groupwork theorists and practitioners in the 1990s is to develop a truly anti-discriminatory methodology.

A fourth trend is the beginning of a shift from a rather insular 'British' perspective on groupwork – and indeed on social work as a whole – to closer links with European colleagues and groupwork developments in their countries. This is primarily part of the wider political 'Europeanisation' but there are some signs of specific groupwork progress. One of these is a special European issue of *Groupwork*

(Heap, 1989) and another is the inception of what are anticipated to be annual European Groupwork Symposia, the first having been held in London in 1991.

Notwithstanding all these positive trends we are still at a very early stage in the development of research into, and formal evaluation of, groupwork. The research-based case for groupwork is no more proven, but certainly no less so, than that for casework. Because of the complexity of researching groupwork practice, and of mounting comparative studies, it will be a long time before definitive research evidence becomes available. Even then, it will probably only be useful at a level of sophistication which discriminates between different methods of groupwork, matched to particular needs, user groups and objectives. There are however some straws in the wind, particularly across the Atlantic. The former journal *Small Group Behaviour* has been renamed *Small Group Research* and under the editorship of Charles Garvin is more oriented towards social groupwork than its predecessor. Also in North America there is now an organisation concerned solely with groupwork research and its dissemination. One of the big debates is the pros and cons of quantitative and qualitative research methods. The small UK-based literature on groupwork research includes material on evaluation methods (Caddick, 1983; Preston-Shoot, 1988) and articles on quantitative methods (Birrell-Weisen, 1991; and from Israel, Cwikel and Oron, 1991). I anticipate that significant progress will be made in our understanding of qualitative methods in the coming years, including illuminative evaluation techniques (Gordon, 1992).

In the absence of major research data, those of us who are committed to the development of groupwork as a method of intervention to stand on at least equal terms with other methods, base our commitment mainly on subjective criteria, 'soft' evaluation techniques, our values and personal experience. For example, I know personally that some groups can be a very effective context and means of help for some individuals, because I have experienced this potency at first hand. As a group member, I have been helped with my own painful and difficult personal problems on several occasions, and I have facilitated or co-worked with numerous groups in which I have witnessed the efficacy of the group as a context in which people can help each other, develop skills and solve problems. This group capacity for empowerment extends beyond mutual aid within the group to individual and group influence in the wider commmunity and organisational systems (see Chapter 6). Follow-up studies and consumer feedback confirm this conviction at a subjective level, as do many journal articles which attempt to evaluate a particular group's 'success'. (Those which 'fail' are rarely written about, but may be equally illuminating!) Also, as outlined elsewhere in this chapter, the unique peer-relationships aspect of the group setting creates a whole range of potential benefits.

I do not see groupwork as a social work panacea however, and the following pages indicate both its potential and its hazards. It will be shown that groupwork is an umbrella term for a wide range of activities, actions and therapies, and that there are certain basic concepts and skills which can be relatively easily acquired by the practitioner who wishes to extend her or his repertoire of creative response to complex human need.

What is groupwork?

Most books on groupwork begin with a detailed analysis of definitions, firstly of the term 'small group' and then of the term 'groupwork'. For the purpose of this book we shall assume that readers share some common notion of what a small group is, but that there is more confusion about what is meant by groupwork. We shall therefore dispose rapidly of the former by taking E.J. Thomas's (1967) working definition of a small group as 'a collection of individuals who are interdependent with one another and who share some conception of being a unit distinguishable from other collections of individuals'. This covers the key concepts of *a defined membership*, *interdependence* and *boundary* ('distinguishable' implies some boundary). We need to add the size of the collection of individuals, which for a small group would normally be thought of as in the range 3–12 persons, and the notion that groups exist for some purpose, however ill-defined.

Before defining groupwork, it is useful to be aware of the range of groups with which social workers may be involved.

These can be represented diagrammatically by 7 circles (see Fig. 1.1, page 7).

The three circles (1–3) above the horizontal line refer to the range of groups with which this book is most directly concerned. They are groups in which the social worker is working directly with group members, and in some acknowledged leadership or resource role. Every group has three levels of focus: individual, group and social environment, but the three circles indicate where the main emphasis lies. This is inevitably an over-simplification, because as McCaughan (1978) has pointed out, the focus of the same group may shift over the duration of its existence.

The four circles (4–7) below the line refer to other work groups with which the social worker may be involved, often in a member role. They are not the direct concern of this book, but some of the principles and processes outlined here for user groups are paralleled in social worker and agency groups. This is illustrated by the vertical positioning of the circles with the work groups paralleling the individual (= social worker), small group (= social work team) and community (= agency/inter-agency) levels. These parallels are not just of academic interest. Experience suggests that where social workers themselves collaborate effectively in groups, and in the social work team in particular, they are more likely to be group-oriented in their work with users, and conversely.

Two contrasting examples illustrate this.

Example: This is a team in name only. Each social worker functions quite separately, protective of their own caseload which they rarely discuss with team colleagues. Their method of working is based on individual and family casework. Team meetings are infrequent and restricted to administrative matters. There is no groupwork and an attempt by two trainees to introduce it is unsuccessful because a group-oriented culture which includes sharing clients is alien to the prevailing ethos.

Example: This team has had the same membership for two years. Over this period a culture of sharing and mutual trust has been developed. Team meetings are frequent and include sharing of work problems, mutual evaluation and feedback, and creative discussion of new developments and ways of working. Groupwork of several kinds – adolescent groups, women's groups, family therapy and various community projects – are

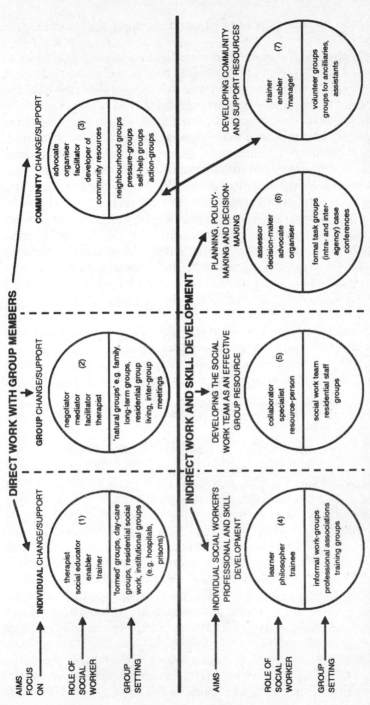

Fig. 1.1 Groups in social work differentiated by aims, the role of the social worker and group setting

DIRECT WORK WITH GROUP MEMBERS

AIMS
FOCUS
ON

INDIVIDUAL CHANGE/SUPPORT

GROUP CHANGE/SUPPORT

COMMUNITY CHANGE/SUPPORT

ROLE OF
SOCIAL
WORKER

therapist
social educator (1)
enabler
trainer

negotiator
mediator (2)
facilitator
therapist

advocate
organiser (3)
facilitator
developer of
community resources

GROUP
SETTING

'formed' groups, day-care
groups, residential social
work, institutional groups
(e.g. hospitals,
prisons)

'natural groups' e.g. family,
long-term groups,
residential group
living, inter-group
meetings

neighbourhood groups
pressure-groups
self-help groups
action-groups

INDIRECT WORK AND SKILL DEVELOPMENT

AIMS

INDIVIDUAL SOCIAL WORKER'S
PROFESSIONAL AND SKILL
DEVELOPMENT

DEVELOPING THE SOCIAL
WORK TEAM AS AN EFFECTIVE
GROUP RESOURCE

PLANNING, POLICY-
MAKING AND DECISION-
MAKING

DEVELOPING COMMUNITY
AND SUPPORT RESOURCES

ROLE OF
SOCIAL
WORKER

learner
philosopher (4)
trainee

collaborator
specialist (5)
resource-person

assessor
decision-maker (6)
advocate
organiser

trainer
enabler (7)
'manager'

GROUP
SETTING

informal work-groups
professional associations
training groups

social work team
residential staff
groups

formal task groups
(intra- and inter-
agency) case
conferences

volunteer groups
groups for ancilliaries,
assistants

integral parts of the team programme. The social workers often work in pairs and sometimes three or four are involved in different roles with members of the same family.

The reader may like to consider how many of these seven types of groups you are currently involved with, and in what roles. Also relevant is your 'invisible' eighth circle which represents the internalised personal reference groups such as family of origin, peer and social groups. These personal groups influence the roles taken and the feelings experienced in group situations at work. Terms such as 'client', 'user' or 'group member' do not distinguish a separate category of persons, but indicate a role which any one of us may take at any time. 'The doer of the Golden Rule, and s/he who is done by, is the same person, is wo/man.' (Erikson, adapted to gender-neutral language).

Definitions of groupwork

One of the most quoted definitions of groupwork against which to set the discussion so far is that developed by Konopka (1963): 'Social groupwork is a method of social work which helps individuals to enhance their social functioning through purposeful group experiences, and to cope more effectively with their personal, group or community problems.'

This definition makes a number of basic points: groupwork is a method of social work; it helps individuals with their social functioning; it is purposeful; it is concerned with coping, at personal, group and community levels.

The emphasis is, however, the rather traditional one of helping the individual with a problem. Contemporary groupwork emphasises action and influence as well as reaction and adaptation. The definition becomes more comprehensive if we add: groupwork provides a context in which *individuals help each other*; it is a method of *helping groups* as well as helping individuals; and it can enable individuals and groups to *influence* and *change* personal, group, organisational and community problems.

There are several difficulties about defining the boundaries of what we call 'groupwork'. The term 'social groupwork' is used by Konopka and others to describe groupwork with an emphasis on *social functioning*, and to distinguish it from *group therapy*, where the emphasis is on emotional needs and psychological processes. Psychotherapeutic groups are included in this text under the term 'groupwork' because there are many similarities with other forms of groupwork, and many social workers work with this type of group. Another boundary problem arises over family therapy – work with the family as a group – because this archetypal 'natural' group has much in common with other kinds of social work groups, but also much that is unique. Family therapy is excluded here because it is a social work method in its own right, and the reader is referred to introductory books by Gorrell-Barnes (1984), Treacher and Carpenter (1984) and Burnham (1986).

Perhaps the most difficult boundary to define is that within the overlap area between groupwork and community work. Social work with community groups can be regarded as a form of groupwork when the groups are relatively small and neighbourhood-centred, but not when more macro, societal and political approaches are used, as in community organisation.

Lastly, training and support groups for volunteers (see Fig. 1.1) and group supervision groups for staff have much in common with some forms of direct groupwork with users.

The practice guidelines in this book are intended to apply to a wide range of groups, but the emphasis will tend to be on formed groups, that is groups which have been specially composed for some purpose. This is because the author's own experience has been mostly in this area, and many of the groups with which social workers are concerned are specially formed ones. However, Chapter 5 specifically considers the kinds of groups and looser groupings which are found in residential and day centres.

Aims of groupwork

The aims of groupwork are many, but before attempting any classification, there are two important questions which should be considered. Firstly, *whose aims are they?* The agency, the social worker, the group members and the community will all have different perspectives on what the same group is for. (An example is given in Chapter 2.)

Secondly, *how explicit are the aims?* Are they overt (disclosed), covert (known, but not disclosed) or unconscious (not known at the time)? One reason for trying to be clear about aims in any group is to minimise the 'hidden agenda'.

One of the best known classifications of groupwork models, by aims, is that by Papell and Rothman (1966). They distinguish the *remedial, reciprocal* and *social goals* models, whose aims are respectively individual social adaptation, mediation between individuals and society (those social agencies which impinge on them directly) and increased social justice. These three aims correspond quite closely to the three levels of focus identified in Fig. 1.1. Each also indicates its own value emphasis.

> *Example*: A group for parents of children 'at risk'. With a 'remedial' focus, the aim might be to help the parents change their ways of treating their children. With a 'reciprocal' focus the aim could be to see how the parents and the groupworker might influence the child welfare agency to provide day care facilities, and how the parents with help might organise themselves into a mutual support system to be called on as a safety-valve at times of stress. With a 'social goals' focus the aim might be improved social and housing conditions for disadvantaged families in the area.

The Papell and Rothman categories are not specific enough for practice purposes, and a more detailed classification of aims is needed. The following is suggested, working from the individual to the societal levels, and bearing in mind that some categories may often overlap and be combined.

(a) *Individual assessment.* These groups are primarily for the assessment of individual needs/abilities/behaviour. The assessment data comes from a combination of self-assessment, worker-assessment and peer-assessment, the latter being the essential group ingredient. Such groups may be used with, for instance, prospective foster parents; adult or juvenile offenders; new admissions to, or prospective discharges from, residential establishments.

(b) *Individual support and maintenance.* These are groups designed primarily to support individuals facing difficult personal or social circumstances. They include, for example, groups for people with a disability themselves (e.g. adolescents with a learning disability), and groups for those who care for them (e.g. their parents, who are in what Whitaker (1985, p.75) calls a 'linked-fate' relationship). Sometimes external aims emerge, e.g. to obtain better day centre facilities for the adolescents.

(c) *Individual change*. This large category includes different (and overlapping) kinds of individual change, ranging from specific behaviours to personal development:

– *social control* e.g. a group for sex offenders to avoid future offending
– *socialisation* e.g. a group to enable institutionalised people to learn social skills for living in a community setting
– *interpersonal behaviour* e.g. assertiveness training groups
– *personal attitudes and values* e.g. a group for drug abusers to influence their attitudes to 'pushing'
– *material circumstances* e.g. a group for unemployed men with the aim of finding work; or a welfare rights group
– *self-concept and feelings* e.g. a group to raise the self-esteem of oppressed minorities; to empower.
– *personal growth and development* e.g. an encounter or 'T' group

(d) *Educational, information-giving and training groups*. For example, groups on welfare rights, parenting, health education, volunteering.

(e) *Leisure/compensatory*. The aim of these groups is to provide individuals with leisure pursuits/enjoyable experiences to compensate for lacks in their personal lives.

(f) *Mediation between individuals and social systems*. These groups involve reciprocal transactions between individuals and social agencies, with change expected 'on both sides' (Schwartz, 1971), e.g. a psychiatric hospital discharge group in which the social worker mediates between individual patients, social service agencies and the hospital authorities to facilitate the return to outside living.

(g) *Group change and/or support*. These are mostly natural or existing groups where the aims are primarily at the group level, e.g. a family group to improve family communication; work with a delinquent gang to divert their energies into more acceptable activities; a residential group to improve the quality of group living.

(h) *Environmental change*. This type of group attempts to

influence the members' social environment, e.g. a residents' group to develop leisure facilities or oppose a road development; a single parents' group to press for day care facilities for the children of working parents.

(i)   *Social change.* These groups aim at social and political change, raising individual consciousness and redistributing power from institutional systems, e.g. local government, to the people. This is a controversial aim in a statutory agency and it falls outside some people's definition of groupwork. Like its polar opposite, social control of individual behaviour, it has overt political purposes and values.

In terms of the Papell and Rothman classification, the aims of categories (a) and (c) are broadly remedial; (b) may start remedial but change later; (f) and (g) emphasise reciprocity, and (h) and (i) are concerned with social goals. Whether groups in categories (d) and (e) are social groupwork or are simply groups of people learning/playing together, will depend on whether the group process is consciously regarded as a significant and important part of what happens.

Heap (1977) has suggested six principal aims of groupwork: alleviating isolation; promoting social learning and maturation; preparing for an approaching crisis or other life change; solving or clarifying problems at the personal/familial level; solving or clarifying problems in the members' environment; achieving insight.

Why and when groupwork?

Some of the aims of groupwork, particularly those concerned with individual change and support, could be (and mostly are) pursued at the casework level. What is the distinctive feature of a group approach, and what are its potential advantages and disadvantages compared with other approaches?

There are some agencies in Britain, and many in the USA, which offer a range of alternative methods, and the service user can choose which to opt for, or take more than one in combination. Even when choice is offered, the intake social worker has some responsibility to advise and give information to facilitate the choice. What evidence and knowledge is available to guide these decisions and choices?

Research findings from social psychology (e.g. Sherif and Sherif, 1969) clearly indicate that under certain conditions individual behaviour and attitudes are influenced by groups. This information is consistent with ordinary life experience of group membership but it does not necessarily follow that groups created or assisted by social workers are successful in achieving their aims. Direct evidence about the efficacy of groupwork compared to other methods or non-intervention is sparse and inconclusive, drawing on a few studies, mainly in the psychiatric setting, and all bedevilled by methodological problems. McCaughan (1978) was unable to include in her reader a chapter on research into groupwork outcome because of the shortage of material. She mentioned a few studies (e.g. *The Wincroft Youth Project*, Smith *et al.*, 1972) as 'some positive evidence for the effectiveness of groupwork', and others in the early 1970s included the work by staff at the University of Michigan (Glasser, Sarri and Vinter, 1974, Chapters 20–29). Studies in the psychiatric field (e.g. Parloff and Dies, 1977) gave some indication that a combined individual and group approach may be more effective for some 'patients' than either method alone. The more recent research referred to above on page 4 does not yet provide anything definitive empirically, but there are likely to be significant developments in the coming decade, particularly in qualitative research such as the *illuminative* approach (Gordon, 1992).

The following guidelines are based therefore on general information about groups, practice experience and subjective evaluation.

Some potential advantages of the groupwork method

Much social living is experienced in groups.   This is apparent in the family, at work and in leisure activities. A natural group *is* real life, and a created group provides a setting where problems of interpersonal relationships and social skills can be worked on at first hand. The skills can then be transferred to natural settings.

Groups of people with similar needs can be a source of mutual support and problem-solving.   People in painful and difficult situations, e.g. spouses of stroke patients, sexually abused children, people with agoraphobia, parents of autistic children, often feel completely alone and different. A social worker can reassure an individual that many others feel like her and know just what it is like, but when this is experienced directly in a group of similarly placed people it carries greater conviction. There is the relief of discovering that one's feelings are 'normal', and the example and advice of others about how to cope.

Attitudes, feelings and behaviour may be changed in a group situation.   This can occur through *social interaction*, including *role-modelling, reinforcement, feedback* and the range of ideas available to each member.

> *Example*: An alcoholic, teetering on the brink of attempting sobriety, meets in an Alcoholics Anonymous (AA) group other alcoholics who have been where she has been, who know the hell and the conflict which she is experiencing, and are now recovered and leading fulfilling lives.

> *Example*: The lone father, whose wife left him 3 months ago, and who feels depressed and desperate, meets other lone fathers who have been separated longer and have developed new life-styles and ways of coping. They are a living proof that change is possible for him too.

In these examples group members role-model personal change and problem-solving, reinforce each other by mutual support and positive feedback, and extend the range of possibilities by sharing different ideas and ways of coping. A prerequisite for change is therapeutic optimism, a belief that change is possible and that there is hope. A group can provide this kind of climate, which can be used constructively or destructively.

In a group, every member is a potential helper.   The roles of social worker and 'client' are significantly less differentiated in a group, because much of the helping and the leadership comes from members of the group, and the social worker is more exposed as a person. Groups can reveal hidden strengths and potential in individuals who have become habituated to labels such as 'useless' and 'inadequate'.

A group can be democratic and self-determining, giving more power to the 'client'. This is the political corollary of mutual helping. Unlike in a one-to-one interview, a person in the role of group member has numerical compensation from her peers for her weaker role position *vis-à-vis* the worker. If there is consensus among group members they are in a powerful position to influence the social worker and the agency. This is one of the reasons why groupwork is viewed with apprehension by some social workers and some agencies. It is a major attraction for those who favour a more participatory, empowering and activist model of social work intervention.

A group setting is particularly suitable for some users of services. There are some people who find the intensity and intimacy of a one-to-one relationship very difficult to cope with, and are much more comfortable in a group of peers. This is true for many adolescents who feel threatened by individual encounters with adults in authority.

Groupwork may be more economical of social worker time and effort. This is a frequently used argument of doubtful validity, especially in formed groups where the social worker is involved in all the preparatory work creating the conditions for the group to take place. In residential and day centre settings, where group members are physically already available, there may be economies of time and effort, depending on how much energy is consumed maintaining space for the group in the larger institution.

A glance at some of the practice-based articles in the journal *Groupwork*, for example one on a group for parents of children with a congenital progressive terminal illness (Engebrigtsen and Heap, 1988), and another for women refugee and asylum seekers (Tribe and Shackman, 1989), provides often moving accounts of what carefully prepared and skilfully run groups can offer people in distress.

Some potential disadvantages of the groupwork method

Confidentiality is more difficult to maintain than in one-to-one work. In a group, by definition, you share yourself and information about you with more people, and the risk of confidentiality being breached is that much greater, particularly as most of the people are not bound by a professional ethic. Some group agreement about confidentiality can reduce but not remove the risk. (Confidentiality is discussed in more detail towards the end of this chapter.)

'Formed' groups are complex to plan, organise and implement. The work involved in preparing this type of group is considerable, and there are often obstacles to overcome at group member, colleague and agency levels.

Groups require resources. The social worker is likely to be involved in negotiations for accommodation, transport, equipment and funds.

X *The individual gets less exclusive attention in a group.* Some individuals, at least at some stages of their development, cannot cope with the sharing and competition involved in a group setting, and need the exclusive attention of an individual relationship. In a group they may be very disruptive, passive, hurt or scapegoated. Sometimes a period of individual work can be a preparation for group participation.

Group membership can increase labelling and stigma. Certain types of groups sometimes attract labels, e.g single-parents group, school-refusers group, sexual abuse perpetrators group, alcoholics group, schizophrenics group, control of violence group. Some people's primary need is 'normalisation' and the last thing they want is a group identity reinforcing their stigmatised label. The name of a group needs careful thought, and neutral titles such as 'Wednesday group' can reduce the danger of stigma.

Groups may be damaging for a small minority. This is not so much a disadvantage of groupwork as a reason for protecting people from being placed in unsuitable groups, and for selecting groupworkers carefully. Lieberman, Yalom and Miles (1973) and Galinsky nd Schopler (1977) have both produced some evidence that some people can be damaged in experiential groups. Their findings are discussed in the section on values and ethics (page 27).

Groupwork or family therapy?

There are, of course, other alternatives to groupwork besides one-to-one casework, notably work with couples and family therapy. In some situations family therapy is not practicable, either because the 'client' is not a member of an available family, or the family is not prepared to approach problems on a group basis. But there will be many cases where there is a genuine choice to be made between the two methods by the social worker and the service users.

As far as I am aware, no clear differential criteria have been established by family therapy and groupwork practitioners or researchers. One indicator is the extent to which the problem faced by an individual appears to be symptomatic of dysfunction in the whole family as a system, and the extent to which it is idiosyncratic to the individual and/or related to other systems such as school, work, and peer groups. One of the few published attempts to make a comparative study (Roman, 1976) indicates that choices tend to be made on the basis of the practitioner's personal philosophy and conceptual framework (focused around the primacy or otherwise of the family group) rather than on any established criteria.

One interesting approach offers 'couples groups' in which several couples facing similar difficulties meet together as a group, thus combining features of both methods. Selection of methods needs careful consideration, and they may be effective in combination, e.g. an ex-psychiatric hospital patient may have family therapy for working at family adjustments on his return, and also attend a social skills group to develop his ability to cope in the community. Alternatively, if he has no family, he may need individual support sessions to gain the confidence to join a group.

What is it like being a social worker doing groupwork?

There are some special features of groupwork which will affect those social workers who practise it.

(*a*) A high level of commitment is necessary for the social worker who is worker or co-worker. It is relatively easy (though not necessarily desirable!) to postpone a commitment with one individual or even a family, but what if a group of ten people are expecting you on an off day?

(b)   Much effort and careful thought needs to go into planning.

(c)   Groupwork is pro-active, in the sense that a positive professional initiative is usually involved, i.e. groupwork does not just happen, as casework can, it has to be initiated.

(d)   Groupwork is more visible to others than one-to-one work, and tends to attract proportionately more attention in the agency. This sometimes results in higher expectations of 'success' than those applied to less visible individual work.

(e)   Groupwork tends to arouse more anxiety in the worker and the agency. The notion of having to obtain permission tends to apply more.

(f)   Groupwork involves sharing, both by users and by social workers and their colleagues.

(g)   Groupwork often highlights technical and values issues which are present, but less obvious, in casework, e.g. contract, manipulation, self-disclosure, recording.

(h)   Groupwork is often exciting and rewarding, especially when the latent potential in individuals is manifest.

Models of groupwork practice

Theoretical influences

Theoretical approaches to groupwork have been influenced by a range of theories contributing to our understanding of group behaviour, e.g. social psychology, criminology, sociology, psychoanalytic theory, learning theory, cognitive frameworks, systems theory and humanistic psychology. Equally important have been practitioners' conceptualisations of practice-theory based on their own experience, creativity and responses to human need and agency function. Group dynamics concepts are not considered in a theoretical way in this text, and the reader is referred to Cartwright and Zander's classic (1968), and to P. Smith's more recent book (1980). For summaries of theories and research findings especially relevant to groupwork, see Hartford (1971), Douglas (1970) and Heap (1977).

The term 'groupwork' subsumes a diversity of approaches to working with groups and a number of different practice models have been developed, principally in North America, but more recently also in the UK. These models tend to overlap and there is not as yet any generally accepted or tidy way of classifying them (Roberts and Northen, 1976).

The *practical usefulness* of any approach is basic to its acceptability, and this will depend, *inter alia*, on the level of skill needed, whether it produces desired results (effectiveness), its cost in resources and how acceptable it is likely to be to both users and agency. Some groupwork beginners prefer the security of following a particular model or approach initially, whereas others like to start eclectically, drawing on a combination of concepts, principles and intuitive response to a particular need. Whatever the approach adopted, it is desirable to have some general idea of what you and the group are trying to achieve, the methods to be used and the underlying assumptions. There are several key variables which every group needs to address, whether it is based on a recognisable model of the kind outlined below, or whether it is simply the worker's own 'model'. These variables are:

(1) *clientele or population* – who is the group for?
(2) *setting* – what is the organisational and physical context of the group?
(3) *needs* – what need(s) is the group attempting to meet?
(4) *aims* – what is the group trying to achieve?
(5) *values* – what values and assumptions underlie this group approach?
(6) *theory* – what theoretical perspectives are being used?
(7) *practice methods* – how is the group membership determined? how is the group structured? what is the role of the worker(s)? how is responsibility shared between worker(s) and members? what is the relative emphasis on the individual, the group and the external environment? what kind of programme/activities/methods are used?

The 'mainstream' models of social groupwork

These are models at the core of the social groupwork tradition (Papell and Rothman, 1980). Two of the classic and seemingly polarised earlier formulations (both usefully summarised and contrasted in Shaffer and Galinsky, 1974) are the *Michigan* (or Vinter) model and the *Schwartz* 'reciprocal' model. The former emphasises contract, programme specificity, outcome and evaluation: leadership is directive and active. The latter emphasises reciprocity, the group as a mutual aid system, and gives primacy to group process: the worker negotiates the programme with the members as the group develops. Both these models have followers in groupwork in Britain (see for example Derricourt and Penrose, 1984, and Cooper, 1980, respectively), Schwartz more so than Vinter, but in recent years other models have been developed.

Papell and Rothman (1966) made the initial breakthrough in models classification with their recognition that models tended to cluster into three categories according to aims: remedial, reciprocal and social goals. Then in an important later article (Papell and Rothman, 1980) they attempted to identify the core elements in contemporary 'mainstream' groupwork, commenting that 'the conception of the group as a mutual aid system has become a universal one in all groupwork practice'. They went on to identify the following factors as other core elements: negotiation of agreed goals between members and worker; spontaneously evolving group processes as the instrumental means for realising group purpose; externality (the external environment); the importance of group development; the encouragement of indigenous leadership roles and increasing group autonomy; and the great diversity of types of group and target population to be served.

These mainstream characteristics provide a useful yardstick when considering the following clusters of models which have been developed, several of them in Britain. My 'classification' is inevitably somewhat arbitrary, but it does clarify some of the major differences in aims and in theoretical and practice emphasis.

(1) *Intake (assessment/induction) models* (Brown and

Seymour, 1983; Hankinson and Stephens, 1985; Todd and Barcome, 1980). These models are relatively easily distinguished because their aims are primarily concerned with the intake process when an individual first engages with an agency, and not with specific interventions such as the provision of support, achievement of change or the amelioration of particular conditions. They are concerned in varying degrees with *group methods of individual assessment* (focus on users) and *induction* (orientation to agency function). These kinds of groups have been used with offenders at the start of their probation or supervision orders, with prospective foster parents, in various residential settings, and in 'walk-in' crisis centres. They have potential for use with a wide range of user groups and in a wide range of settings. They do however need to be distinguished from specialised types of treatment, change or action groups which a person may enter at referral when their particular need is already clear and accepted by all concerned.

(2) *Guided group interaction models* (Stephenson and Scarpitti, 1974). These social control models aim to change delinquent and anti-social behaviour into law-abiding and socially responsible behaviour (sic). The theoretical basis is sociological/criminological and asserts that as peer groups often provide the context for learning deviant behaviour, attitudes and values, then by using the same process in reverse, carefully constituted peer groups can be a vehicle for changing behaviour from the anti-social to the law-abiding. The key principle is to mix offenders with ex-offenders, the latter exerting positive peer group pressure on the former (Cressey, 1955). The group culture is one of openness and the methods used are highly confrontational as well as highly supportive.

The settings are often residential or day centre establishments and these programmes are exemplified in *positive peer culture* (Vorrath and Brendtro, 1984) and the Phoenix-House model for drug abusers. Both apply similar peer-confrontation principles. Some intermediate treatment groups (in Britain) at the 'heavy' end use this form of peer-pressure combined with cognitive/behavioural methods. Apart from the philosophical and ethical issues raised, there are problems about sustaining change when the person returns to his or her own social network, if the peer-pressure there is anti- rather than pro-social.

(3) *Problem-solving, task-centred and social-skills models.* This group of models takes in quite a wide range of 'structured' approaches, all characterised by the aim of solving specific behavioural problems, achieving specific tasks or developing specific behavioural skills. The behavioural emphasis is in the Michigan groupwork tradition (see for example Garvin, Reid and Epstein's task-centred groupwork model, 1976, and Rose's work on behavioural group methods, 1978, 1980). By contrast, the social skills and personal problem-solving model developed by Priestley, McGuire *et al.* (1978) combines a structured, highly programmed approach with humanistic values. Their model is based on the four stages of assessment, setting objectives, learning, and evaluation. An individual's perception and definition of their own problem is the starting point, with a high expectation of successful problem-solving and skill-development. It is not exclusively a group approach as it uses a blend of individual, pairs and group methods.

More recently there has been a growing interest in the explicit use of cognitive and social learning models and methods (see for example Goldstein, 1988 and Ross *et al.*, 1986). Practitioners have of course been using cognitive techniques implicitly for many years.

(4) *Time-limited 'mainstream' groups in the UK statutory context.* The mainstream model in the contemporary British context was described in an article entitled 'Towards a British model of groupwork' (Brown, Caddick, Gardiner and Sleaman, 1982). The essential elements of this approach, which is practised quite widely in Social Services and Probation Departments, and in some voluntary agencies with quasi-statutory functions, were summarised as: 'individual-centred aims consistent with meeting client need and carrying out agency function; an eclectic theoretical base; an overall approach which values peer sharing and mutual feedback; the creative use of a range of group techniques; co-leadership; a closed membership of from six to twelve adults (usually strangers initially, but sharing similar problems) and time-limited duration'. These groups, typical of many written up in the British social work journals

at that time, are conceptualised in a way which recognises that they are significantly affected in their process by the organisational context and the limited time available.

(5) *Psychotherapeutic person-focused models.* These models are characterised by their common concern with the person and their emotions, feelings and relationships. They share the aim of strengthening an individual's mental health and self-concept, but the methods used and the theoretical underpinning vary considerably from psychoanalytic group therapies (e.g. Slavson, 1943) to here-and-now methods such as gestalt, psychodrama and transactional analysis – see below – based on humanistic 'growth' psychologies and self-actualisation philosophies. Yalom's book on group psychotherapy (1985 edn) offers a rich source of group therapy concepts and techniques of direct relevance to social groupwork. Some practitioners find Whitaker and Lieberman's focal conflict theory very helpful (1964).

Gestalt therapy (Perls, 1971) is a demanding here-and-now therapy using the 'hot seat' technique in which an individual is enabled to get in touch with immediate problematic experience and emotion, and work through the conflict or *impasse*. Other group members are involved indirectly via identification, reassurance and support. A groupworker would need specialist training to take the therapist's role, as they would in the following two therapies.

Psychodrama (Blatner, 1973; Gale, 1990) is a dynamic approach designed to evoke the expression of feelings involved in personal problems in a spontaneous, dramatic, role-play. The main thrust of the method is to help participants relive and reformulate their problems in dramatic form in order to face their concerns directly and immediately in the living present. Experience in action, rather than words, is the touchstone. Psychodrama is a group-based model, with transferable techniques of direct use to groupworkers (see Chapter 4 which also describes *sociodrama*).

Transactional analysis (Pitman, 1984) is an example of a specific technique developed with individuals, but now often practised in groups. The basic concept of the parent-adult-child ego-structure is quickly grasped, and like psychodrama, it is a technique which can be drawn on and practised at whatever level the practitioner has reached. The potential of TA has not yet been fully developed as a group technique, the group often being little more than an arena for individual 'work'.

(6) *Self-help, mutual support models* (Silverman, 1980; Brimelow and Wilson, 1982; Habermann, 1990). This type of group is largely self-governing and provides its members with a source of mutual help and support. Alcoholics Anonymous is an example of a long-established fully autonomous self-help group. There has been a rapid growth of self-help groups in recent years covering almost every kind of human need, including: socially oppressed minorities e.g. black women's groups; shared health problems e.g. mastectomy groups, agoraphobia groups; 'linked-fate' groups (Whitaker, 1985) e.g. carers' groups, parents of children with learning difficulties; consumers of social services groups e.g. NAYPIC (National Association for Young People in Care), foster parents' groups – the list is endless.

There are also some 'in-between' or quasi self-help groups where the social worker has some role-relationship with the group at least for a while. This role may involve her in *negotiating* with agencies and others for resources on behalf of the group, *mediating* between members, *facilitating* the development of group cohesion, *clarification* of roles, *conflict-resolution*, acting as *consultant*, and many other roles. In an article entitled 'Self-Help Groups: a Minefield for Professionals', Habermann (1990), writing in the Danish context, identifies and analyses the often ambivalent and fraught relationship that can develop between professional workers and self-help groups. Brimelow and Wilson (1982) provide a useful guide to steps that can be taken to make this sensitive relationship as effective as possible.

(7) *Social goals/social action/self-directed models*. The particular feature of this cluster of models, which in the past have been developed mostly in the youth and community work context (see Button, 1974; Thomas, 1978), is their concern with goals external to the group and with some form of social development and social change. The models can be differentiated according to their emphasis on *process* (the effect group participation itself has on the members) or *product* (practical gains which the group achieves e.g. some

new neighbourhood resource), and according to the degree of *politicisation* and *structural change* associated with both aims and methods. Button's model is an example of *developmental groupwork*, focused on 'ordinary' children and adolescents in their own community setting. Community action groups, more akin to community work, are neighbourhood groups which identify and work to achieve defined environmental changes, e.g. tenants' associations pressing for children's play facilities.

Mullender and Ward (1991) have recently conceptualised a *self-directed* model of groupwork. This model derives from practice and has been developed and refined in close association with groupwork practitioners and users of services. It places a strong emphasis on *empowerment* as the core principle (see next section), and whilst containing elements of more traditional social groupwork methods, it is most clearly distinguished by a combination of external goals and member self-directedness. Thus the role of the worker is defined and conceptualised as 'facilitator' rather than 'leader' (Ward and Mullender, 1991). Examples of self-directed groups for a range of users (young people in care, adolescent offenders, parents of children on the child protection register, women's groups, Asian young people, people with disabilities, older people in residential care, mental health patients) are given in the main text (Mullender and Ward, 1991). Badham *et al.* (1988) have published an account of the use of this method with young offenders. One of the interesting questions raised by this model is whether in the statutory context it can be reconciled with agency social control objectives.

(8) *Empowerment models.* In the last decade increasing attention has been given to group models which have empowerment at the heart. There is an obvious overlap with the social goals models of the previous section – particularly the self-directed model – but whereas social goals models have derived mostly from the youth, community and settlement tradition, there is another source of conceptualisation of empowerment groups deriving from the response to the oppression of women, black people and other oppressed groups. Much of the published material on this development

on both sides of the Atlantic is by women writing about women's groups and feminist groupwork (see for example Breton, 1989 and 1991; Lee, 1991; Butler and Wintram, 1991). A central theme in these conceptualisations is the development of a practice theory which combines both intra-group response to individual pain and need with collective group action to confront and change external institutions and systems which oppress and diminish group members. (See also Chapter 6 on anti-discriminatory groupwork with particular reference to race and gender.)

Human relations training groups (Smith, 1980)

These groups are concerned with here-and-now 'sensitivity' training for practitioners from various professions whose work involves them in group leadership and membership. They are *not* a social groupwork model to be used in social work agencies when working with users, but are included here because of their value in developing the groupworker's own personal awareness of the less obvious, sometimes unconscious processes which affect all groups and their capacity to carry out their tasks. The value of sensitivity groups as a training experience is discussed in Chapter 7. Models used for this purpose include Tavistock, T-groups and encounter group models, and excellent summaries of these approaches can be found in Shaffer and Galinsky (1974).

Groupwork in residential and day centre settings

Most of the groupwork models outlined above have been developed in 'fieldwork' settings and are not necessarily suitable for direct application in the 'group living' settings of day and residential centres. In these centres each group or grouping of members and staff is part of the whole 'mosaic' of centre life and likely to be profoundly affected by what is going on elsewhere. A whole chapter (5) later in this book analyses what difference this makes to working in and with groups in these settings and offers some guidelines to the special skills needed. (See also Brown and Clough, 1989.)

Summary on models

A wide range of approaches is included loosely under the term 'groupwork' and it is possible to cluster models and methods in various ways. The above classification is one way of identifying some of the major factors which distinguish different groupwork models and methods.

The practice guidelines in the following chapters are not based on one particular model. The emphasis will be on the basic principles, skills and processes which apply to most groups, and which can be adapted by practitioners to suit different settings, styles, needs and values. It is to the latter that we turn in the final section of this chapter.

Values and ethics

A survey of the groupwork literature reveals that with the exception of Bernstein's seminal work (1972) little was written explicitly about groupwork values and ethics until quite recently. Even now values issues tend to be raised indirectly through the elaboration of group methods based on particular ideologies such as self-directed or feminist groupwork. However, every groupworker has a *de facto* if not an explicit personal values stance which will influence groups that he or she works with. As Bernstein states, there is no such thing as value-neutrality in groupwork, or indeed in social work. Every action and communication, whether verbal or non-verbal, says something about the worker's values (and those of the author will no doubt be evident in this book). A central question for every groupworker to ask himself or herself is 'How clear am I about my own values, how do they affect the way I work with others in groups, and how explicitly do I, and can I, share them with those I work with?'

Of course many of the core groupwork values and ethics are those held throughout social work (see for example Watson's edited volume reviewing the BASW code of ethics, 1985). Some however, including confidentiality, self-determination, empowerment, worker-style and group pressure, have a uniquely group dimension. In this section a selection of important groupwork values and ethical issues will be discussed. For a detailed treatment of anti-discriminatory groupwork with particular reference to race and gender equality see Chapter 6.

Art or science?

In his philosophical allegory *Zen and the Art of Motor-Cycle Maintenance*, Pirsig (1976) distinguished two stereotypes of the motorcycle enthusiast. One is the person who is a first-rate mechanic and excels in the technical aspects of motor cycles and their maintenance. He understands how they work and can repair them when they go wrong. As he rides along he is conscious of how well the engine is functioning. This stance is 'classical' or scientific. The second type of motorcyclist gets satisfaction and delight from the experience of riding the machine at speed along country roads on a beautiful day. He feels the air and senses the sounds and smells. If there is a mechanical fault, he takes the bike to the nearest garage. This stance is 'romantic' or artistic.

The social-science equivalents of these two positions are logical positivist and existentialist respectively. In groupwork terms the former is concerned with specific goals, detailed programme, clear roles, defined structure and evaluation of outcome. The latter views the process itself as being of paramount importance, the experience providing its own validation. Each groupworker will be at some point on this science–art continuum. Pirsig's resolution of the apparent art–science conflict is integration at a higher level which he calls 'quality'. In my view, high quality groupwork involves taking an interest in both what people experience *and* what they achieve.

Structural v psychological ideologies

Each social worker has some kind of personal ideology, be it Christian, Zen Buddhist, Humanist, Marxist, Anti-Racist, Feminist or a pragmatic mixture of these and others. Some approaches to groupwork are explicitly linked to a particular ideology (e.g. Butler and Wintram, 1991; Mullender and Ward, 1991), others are more functional. Probably one of the biggest differentiators is between those who espouse a psychological framework and those who draw on a structural analysis as the starting point for their approach. In practice many accept a sociological explanatory framework but fall back on micro-practice methods because the wider canvas seems so daunting and difficult. One of the strengths of prevalent anti-oppressive groupwork ideologies, and feminist groupwork in particular, is that unlike their marxist predecessors they take account of both 'the personal and the political' in developing an explicit practice-theory which is usable by practitioners.

Most ideological perspectives converge on some of the fundamental tenets of social groupwork but with a difference in emphasis. For example, most groupworkers favour the principle of self-determination for group members, but not all take this literally to the point that the members themselves make all the key decisions about group aims, methods and direction. Similarly, every groupworker accepts the core principle of 'mutual aid', but whereas many settle for it at the interpersonal level within the group, others like Breton (1989) say that is not enough and it has to be combined with mutual aid in the form of collective action to confront external discrimination, poverty and structural disadvantage.

Use and abuse of power and control

It is interesting to observe that whilst in one dimension 'person-changing' and 'system-changing' practitioners are at opposite poles, they are both exercising their power to try to influence others, individually or collectively, in directions they desire. How prepared is either of them to be changed themselves by the power of the group and its members?

One social worker, working with a group of boys from a delinquent subculture, was surprised to find over a period of time that instead of the boys' attitudes changing, her own were being changed. To her dismay, she was gradually becoming converted to the logic of their delinquent lifestyle. She complained that no one had warned her about that on her training course! By contrast, in the group therapy scene in *One Flew Over the Cuckoo's Nest* (Kesey, 1973), the nursing sister ruthlessly exercises her institutionally based power to reduce individual patients' power and ensure group conformity on the ward. A more group- and social-action-oriented worker would have 'allowed' the group to be a context for each patient to discover the source and nature of his own and the group's power. This could have led to pressure for changes in the hospital regime and, undoubtedly, the particular hospital depicted so graphically by Ken Kesey would rapidly have sacked the sister or terminated the group in such circumstances!

Agency powers and the empowerment of group members

In Britain an important current debate about groupwork is whether the emphasis on empowerment of group members is compatible with the legislative and administrative powers exercised over individuals by statutory authorities. This issue is, for example, central to groupwork in the fields of child protection and probation. Articles in two special issues of the journal *Groupwork* (Kerslake and Brown, 1990; Brown and Caddick, 1991) include both theoretical discussion and practice illustration of the dilemmas faced.

Two practice accounts, interestingly both about women's groups, one in a Social Services Department and one in Probation, suggest that compatibility is possible under certain circumstances. In the former, Bodinham and Weinstein (1991) describe a group for women from disadvantaged backgrounds which was concerned with empowerment but also had responsibility for monitoring children at risk from non-accidental injury, and undertaking mental health admissions. The (female) workers were open from the beginning about the nature of their statutory power and responsibilities, and on several occasions had to exercise those powers with individual group members. However, this took place in a context where the empathy between women workers and members established a level of trust and confidence which made the authority of the workers 'accountable' to the members. In the second example from probation (Jones *et al.*, 1991) some women probation officers set up a group for women offenders. Unlike previous groups which had marginalised women and/or stereotyped them in the 'welfare' mode, this group took a 'justice' approach tackling the reality of their offending behaviour directly in a way which empowered the women and helped them to be more in control of their own lives and environment.

What is confidential in a group?

There are two ways in which confidentiality can be a special problem in groups. The first, particularly in a statutory agency, concerns what the social worker does with the information about individuals which emerges in a group. Does she pass it on to other colleagues who may have referred the group member, does she record it in the personal file or does she maintain complete secrecy? The second concerns what any one group member does with information about any of the others. Each member has a right to know the answers to these questions, because they will affect freedom to trust, take risks and divulge personal information about oneself or others.

Considering that only the worker is bound by a professional ethic, it is surprising how often confidentiality is respected in groups. This may be because although group members' confidentiality ethic is discretionary rather than absolute, it is often acceptable in the relevant culture. One safeguard is to have open discussions about it at the group contract-making stage, and to establish a working agreement which is accepted by all. When a group session and activities are to be recorded in sound or video, group members' agreement would normally be sought and a clear undertaking given of the purpose of such a recording and the limitations on its use. If an agency requires the worker to pass on certain types of information either verbally or in agency records, then members should know this, and can then act accordingly. Another advantage of making this clear in the contract is that when something very personal or controversial is divulged, members can if necessary be reminded of the agreement. In groupwork, the gains of collective responsibility and mutual helping carry with them the risks of indiscretion and abuse.

Is there a hidden agenda?

Groupwork varies in the extent to which there is an open culture. The style adopted by the worker will often be a role-model for others. The manipulative worker with his hidden agenda cannot expect a group full of open, trusting members! There are many advantages in openness and the onus is on the worker to find very good reasons for any secrecy. There may be occasions when damaged or disturbed people need protection from openness, but the worker needs to consider very carefully whether it is not himself or his agency he is really trying to protect with his hidden agenda (which is not to say that social workers do not have very real needs for protection too). The contract approach discussed in the next chapter reflects the 'open' ethic.

Should group membership always be voluntary?

This is a difficult question facing social workers in statutory agencies. Many of the activities, contacts and decisions in statutory social work involve varying degrees of coercive behaviour by social workers. Is mandatory group membership of a different order of coercion? A young person in a residential home has to do many things required by the staff and the regime, and it could be said that participation in formal groups is no different from playing football, attending craft workshops, maths classes or individual counselling sessions. In a country with compulsory education up to the age of sixteen, this would at least be consistent. But what of the thirty-year-old woman on probation? Should she have more choice about whether she joins a social skills group than whether she meets her probation officer individually? Should she know, when she agrees to be placed on probation, that this is a commitment to participate in some type of activity, but with choice among those available? There are no easy answers to these questions, not least because in many situations the distinction between voluntary and compulsory is blurred. An old lady in an elderly persons' home wants to choose not to take part in group discussions about preparation for death; a fifteen-year-old wants to opt out of a group discussion on personal relationships at an activity camp; a parent of a child on a supervision order would prefer not to join a parent effectiveness group: each might suspect that although a choice is offered, refusal to comply could have adverse consequences and repercussions.

One guiding principle that can be applied generally is maximum clarity and openness about whether there is a real choice about (a) joining or (b) opting out. When people are compelled to join a group this has consequences in the group which are sometimes (but not necessarily always) negative. Mackintosh (1991) writes about a centralised groupwork programme for offenders in a city probation setting in which attendance is genuinely voluntary yet remains between 80 per cent and 90 per cent: higher than attendance in many other settings. As stated above there are of course other pressures on the offenders to attend groups, but nevertheless it is significant that a high level of motivation to attend voluntarily has been achieved by this programme.

Can groups be damaging to individuals?

It is axiomatic that any activity or experience which has potential for beneficial change also has potential for unhelpful or even damaging change. One issue is whether individuals at risk can be identified and protected by exclusion or safeguards. Another is the quality of leadership and acceptability of the method. Most of the research which has been done on the subject (Lieberman, Yalom and Miles, 1973; Galinsky and Schopler, 1977) has been done on T-groups and encounter groups, and often with student populations. This makes generalisation about other types of group and populations problematic.

The study reported by Lieberman *et al.* was on the effects of encounter groups on Stanford students. About 8 per cent of the sample were rated as 'casualties' as a direct result of group participation. The 'mechanisms of injury' included attacks by leader or group; rejection by leader or group; failure to attain unrealistic goals; coercive expectations; and input overload or 'value shuffle'. This research has been criticised on methodological and other grounds but some of the findings may at least serve as pointers to groupworkers in other contexts.

The worker has a responsibility not to attack or reject individuals, but gentle confrontation and almost any intervention can be experienced subjectively by an individual as attack or rejection if she is feeling under pressure or low in self-esteem or perhaps the worker's action triggers some painful past experience. The setting of realistic and achievable goals is desirable, as is sensitivity about challenges to other people's value systems. Care in group composition is another safeguard, but with many groups, whether for ideological or contextual reasons, the worker often has no choice. The positive leadership qualities which minimise the likelihood of damage to individuals are outlined in Chapter 3.

There are no clear answers to most of the values and ethical issues discussed here. Each practitioner faces these issues within the general framework of personal and social work ethics and ideology.

2 Planning a Group: Preparation and Contract

This chapter is about what takes place before the first meeting of a group. The importance of this stage in groupwork cannot be overestimated. Research evidence (Douglas, 1970) and practice experience both testify that effectiveness or 'success' (however defined) are determined as much by what happens before the group comes into existence, as by what happens during the group's life. The preparation stages may lack the demands, enjoyment and involvement of actual group meetings and activities, but they require just as much creative energy, clear thinking and skill in communication. Some groups are stillborn or die later because social workers underestimate the time and care which good preparation requires.

The idea of forming a group, or working with an existing one, usually comes from one or more individuals who may be potential group members, individual social workers, the team or senior agency staff. Whoever first thought of the group is likely to have a special investment in it which will influence the subsequent course of events, during preparation and as the group develops. Another factor will be the reactions of others to the perceived motives of the initiators. Thus preparation for a group is not only a straightforward rational procedure, but a process which is affected by people's feelings and reactions to each other as well as the proposal itself.

Planning and preparation for a group includes three stages, which often overlap. Firstly, the groupworker must be satisfied that a need or problem exists and is shared by a number of people for whom some common aim can be identified. She must also be satisfied that a group is more likely than other available methods to meet the need and achieve the aim. She should be able to commit the outline scheme to paper.

Secondly, the organisational and environmental context of the group must be assessed to see whether there is sufficient support to make the group worth attempting. This 'sounding out' or feasibility study includes preliminary negotiations with persons and groups in the agency (and elsewhere if necessary) who are in influential positions and whose support is needed. These may include management staff who control resources needed for the group, and colleagues whose clients are potential group members.

Thirdly, the actual process of creating the group will be undertaken, if the indications from the previous stages are positive. This stage involves obtaining resources, recruiting a membership and making initial decisions about time, place and duration. It also includes making arrangements for consultation, and negotiating a preliminary contract or working agreement with members.

Perspectives on aims and expectations

The range of possible aims for different groups was outlined in the previous chapter. In a statutory agency there are likely to be differing aims for the same group. Aplin (1977) has distinguished the *agency perspective*, the *practice perspective* and the *user perspective*. These three perspectives will often differ and a viable group requires not that they are identical, but that there are sufficient common elements. It also requires a reasonable convergence of perspective within each category, i.e. as between potential members and as between co-worker(s) and relevant colleagues. The following example illustrates the possible variation in perspectives, even when there is apparently common agreement on needs and goals.

> *Example*: A Social Services Department District Office decides to form a group for lone parents, with an associated playgroup for their children. The aim is stated in general terms as a support group for lone parents to help them manage more easily. Whilst nearly everyone subscribes to this rather vague aim, perceptions of what it really means vary considerably.

The *agency perspective* is influenced by some criticism

about the number of children from one-parent families being taken into care. Funds for preventive work are available under the relevant legislation, and this type of group is seen as an effective form of prevention. It would also be an opportunity to keep a closer watch on several families under suspicion for child abuse, and to make sure that the children get a proper midday meal. The parents could be taught practical things concerned with home management, social skills and caring for the children. The Area Director is keen to have parents' groups in each of her districts, as they are increasing elsewhere in the county and currently favoured by the Department. The team leader is a groupwork enthusiast and sees the group as a way of putting his team on the map as a progressive multi-method unit.

The social workers illustrate the *practice perspective*. They will be directly involved with establishing and running the group, and have various motives for supporting it, including a conviction that groupwork is more effective than casework for helping these families; a wish to increase their own groupwork experience and skills; a belief that having a thriving group will enhance the status of their team; and a hope that they can be more influential with users and improve the standards of child care, emotionally and physically. It will also make a welcome change from the round of home visits, and hopefully establish better relationships with the families.

The *user perspective* is similarly varied. Some of the parents, especially those regularly visited by a social worker, see this group as a new means of checking up on their treatment of their children. They feel under some pressure to join, as the social workers have powers to take their children into care. On the other hand, it would be nice to have the children looked after by someone else one morning a week, and to have the opportunity to sit around and talk with other parents. There is the added attraction of a cheap lunch and free coffee. Some are hoping to make new friends. One hopes that if she attends regularly she may be able to get her eldest child back from the foster parents. Some hope that going to the group will be a support and help them in trying to cope with their children and family responsibilities.

When there is a general aim, as in this example, expectations are more likely to be divergent. One way of attempting to get more consensus about expectations is to be more specific about aims. This will not remove the different perspectives illustrated above, but it can provide a baseline for identifying variations at the contract-making stage when time spent 'clearing expectations' often pays dividends later. This can be repeated at intervals during the life of the group, but becomes less necessary when the members themselves are actively involved in planning and leadership. In some 'reciprocal' approaches, the groupworker is deliberately non-specific about aims at the pre-group stages, leaving scope for the group itself to decide on goals at its first meeting.

The group and its environment

As Whitaker (1976) has stated, 'A group is more likely to be successful if it is conducted in an organisation or institutional context in which other personnel, not directly involved with the group, nevertheless accept and support its aims and general procedures, and value its potential contribution to the shared goals of the institution or organisation.' This means that at a very early stage the social worker has to assess the environmental context of any group she is considering establishing. If there is a positive tradition and wide acceptance of groupwork in the organisation, all is well, and routine procedures are followed. If, on the other hand, groupwork is either new or has to contend with an unhappy past history of organisational indifference or even hostility, then preparation of the environment is essential, and may take a long time and much hard work.

Three organisational settings will now be considered: non-social-work-oriented institutions (with a social work presence); residential and day centres; and fieldwork settings.

*The non-social-work-oriented institution (with a
social work presence)*

Anyone who has attempted groupwork in a prison, hospital or school setting, will be aware of the power of the institutional forces, and how dependent the groupworker is on the co-operation of non-social-work staff. Two examples illustrate this:

Example: The first meeting of a prison group is held in a room on the education wing. The group has been carefully planned and has the approval of the Governor and Chief Officer. The two leaders are sitting waiting for the prison officers to bring the group members from their wing in another part of the prison. No one comes. Eventually one of the leaders, who is a prison welfare officer, sets off angrily to the wing, only to be told on arrival that the prison officers 'didn't know' about the group meeting. At last, the group meeting starts but it gets interrupted by prison officers opening the door from time to time, and staring through the window. When the group ends, the leaders and the members have to run the gauntlet of officers in the passage and a senior officer says in a voice all can hear, 'You're wasting your bloody time with these buggers, they'll never change.' This group survived the test and was allowed to function relatively smoothly thereafter. More significantly, it paved the way for other groups to follow. Some (unpublished) experience in prisons where prison officers are directly involved in leading social skills groups for men approaching discharge, has indicated the potential strength of institutional support and involvement.

Example: A therapy group is suggested in a state psychiatric hospital in the USA with no recent tradition of a group approach. A social worker and a psychologist, both quite recently appointed to the hospital staff, endeavour to start a group therapy programme. This is not approved of by medical staff committed to the individual treatment model, and groups are frequently interrupted when particular patients are 'needed' for dance therapy, injections and other diversionary treatments.

These illustrations, perhaps rather daunting but not particularly unusual, indicate the need to create 'space' for a group in such an institution by preparing the ground carefully and attempting to gain enough support at least to protect the outer boundary of the group from external 'sabotage'. Many people have fantasies and fears about groups and their power, and preparation time spent working through some of these feelings, as well as discussing all the practical and organisational problems, usually pays dividends.

The other extreme to institutional opposition is institutional pro-group policies where the norm is to have groups on all wards, wings or houses. Where this forms part of a coherent, well thought-out therapeutic milieu, as in the prototype of the Henderson hospital (M. Jones, 1953), the environmental support structure is invaluable. Where it is a policy imposed on a largely unwilling staff and residents, it becomes counterproductive and liable to discredit the contribution of groupwork.

Residential and day centres (see Chapter 5)

The significance for groupwork of the group living in an organisational setting of residential and day centres is discussed in detail in Chapter 5. Whether we are thinking of community homes, probation hostels or family centres, any single group activity, formal or informal, will be profoundly affected by the mosaic of other groups and groupings that make up the total living environment. This means that consistency of values, aims and methods throughout the centre is important. Unlike schools, prisons and hospitals, these are establishments over which the personal social services – statutory or voluntary – are likely to have direct control.

Example: In the USA some residential establishments for young offenders have adopted the 'positive peer culture' approach (Vorrath and Brendtro, 1984) which focuses on a set group meeting for one and a half hours each evening, with the rest of the day spent on education, PE, work and leisure activities. The strength of the approach (which can be criticised on other grounds) is that the formal group session is consciously and consistently related to the rest of the entire programme, and vice versa. All the staff (whether teacher, cook, group-worker, PE instructor or director) have a commitment to an integrated approach, so the group meetings, which are primarily based on peer influence, have all the advantages of institutional support and consistency.

The fieldwork setting

Here the influence of the agency environment on a group-work proposal is perhaps less obvious than in an institutional setting, but it can be equally powerful. This is illustrated by the experience of one social work training course which encourages students to seek opportunities to work with groups during a six-month fieldwork placement. A pattern has emerged indicating that whether or not a student gets some groupwork experience on placement is at least as dependent on the prevailing attitudes in the agency and team as it is on the needs and motivation of the users, or the commitment and skills of the students.

The agency environment in general

Indicators of a supportive agency environment for groupwork include the availability of money and other resources; availability of supervision and consultation; recognition of groupwork in workload calculations; collaboration from colleagues in 'sharing' clients, co-working together with groups and providing emotional support; and an agency climate which values social workers using creative means to achieve statutory ends (Laming and Sturton, 1978). These 'ideal' conditions often take years to establish, but if the climate is favourable much can be achieved.

It is not possible to lay down specific procedures or strategies to be followed when groupwork is not widely accepted in an agency or institution, because each context is different, but most approaches include the following:

(*a*)   seeking the support of colleagues in the team;
(*b*)   consulting with middle-managers, enabling them to understand more about your project, express their views and feel involved;
(*c*)   producing written information about the proposed group, its aims and requirements, and how these (e.g. resources, accommodation, shared clients, community involvement) may affect others in the agency;
(*d*)   being sensitive to the feelings of others. Groups are still perceived by many people as rather threatening and mysterious, especially in teams based on traditional casework approaches. It is important that colleagues who prefer other approaches are not made to feel excluded or inferior in status. Open opposition is much easier to respond to than a mixture of verbal support ('I think your group is a good idea') coupled with contradictory actions ('I never seem to have anyone suitable for your group on my caseload').

The above guidelines suggest that a measure of agency

consensus is possible if the necessary groundwork is under-taken. Whilst I believe this to be generally true there will be times when groupwork is undertaken in spite of opposition in some quarters. Groupwork models adopting radical aims, including change in the agency itself, will inevitably have to give more attention to strategy and conflict-resolution.

The social environment

In addition to the agency environment, groups are influenced by the social environment of the participants. All potential workers and members of a social work group are also members of other groups and alliances in their own social settings. Examples of these are families, friendship groups, schoolmates, work groups and gangs. These primary groups constitute part of the social environment systems which influence decisions about group membership and participation.

Example: An activity/social education group for ten- to twelve-year-old children with behaviour difficulties. As this group is to be held during school hours, the groupworkers are dependent on the co-operation of both teachers and parents. The group has much more chance of getting started and becoming useful for each child if it is at least tolerated, if not actively supported, by the primary environments of home and school. If there is opposition, the child is in constant role-conflict about joining the group and attending sessions.

Example: An activity group for young offenders. For the first meeting the probation officer has recruited four members, three who know each other and a fourth, Jim, who is a member of another gang. Halfway through the first session the other members of that gang arrive quite unexpectedly, requesting that Jim leave the group and go with them, which he does meekly before the leader or members can do anything about it.

Example: Two social workers, co-working with a therapeutic group from 6.30 to 8.00 on Monday evenings, are male and female colleagues. The man is single and his girl-friend, being a nurse, understands about evening work (though she wishes he would take time off in lieu!) He gets her support and feels it within him when planning and leading the group. His female colleague is married with two children and feels constantly under pressure because her children expect her home in the evening, and so does her husband (not a social worker) who resents the intimacy of the 'professional marriage' which she and her colleague need for effective co-working with the group. The husband has feelings of exclusion from this social work activity which he cannot really understand and which sometimes seems to him to be more a way of life than a job to be done.

The physical environment

Groups are also affected by the physical environment in which meetings and activities take place. Firstly, there are the connotations a particular room has for each person, e.g. health clinic, pub, probation office, youth club, deaf institute, community centre. Secondly, there is the direct impact of the physical layout and its suitability for a particular purpose. Studies in proxemics (the study of personal and social space) have shown that human communication is much influenced by physical spacing and distance (Hall, 1969). Thirdly, familiar territory has a supportive and reassuring function for a group and changes of territory in mid-group can have an unsettling effect.

Resources and finance

Because groups always involve a number of people and often use activities, they require resources of various kinds. The availability or otherwise of resources says something about the priority groupwork is given by an agency. If groupwork is seen as an integral method of social work intervention, the resources should be there, whereas if it is viewed as an optional extra then the material response is likely to be cheeseparing and reluctant. A basic groupwork skill is that of obtaining the necessary resources. This is not easy, and the agency may directly or indirectly expect the social workers to furnish evidence that the group will be effective and the money well spent. Perhaps because groupwork is more visible than casework, official expectations of pay-off and cost-effectiveness tend to be higher, placing additional pressure on the social workers concerned. Several of the necessary resources for groupwork are considered below.

Time

Groupwork involves considerable expenditure of social worker time and the amount is often underestimated. It appears more economical to see eight people all together than each separately, but the arithmetic is more complicated than that! Firstly, there is the time needed for planning the group, and all the various negotiations that are necessary. Secondly, there is the time involved directly in the sessions themselves. This might be one or two hours each week, plus, in some groups, block periods of weekends or several weekdays for particular activities such as camps, outings, social skills training or therapeutic workshops. A model gaining in popularity in some settings is the three- or four-day continuous group (see for example Mackintosh, 1991). Thirdly, time is needed between sessions for planning, reviewing, recording, obtaining resources, and meeting with a consultant and/or co-worker. Fourthly, time may also be needed between sessions for meeting with group members individually, visiting absentees and other significant persons in their family and social networks.

The total time needed for a group varies widely according to type, but for each group an estimate can be made, allowing for the various extra group commitments. This expenditure of time should be allowed for in exactly the same way as any other work commitments. If groupwork involves evening or weekend work, time needs to be allowed in lieu. This may seem obvious, but often does not happen.

Staff

A groupwork programme, whether in a residential, day centre or community setting, requires staff who are motivated to commit time and skill and to take on leadership roles. Many groups need two workers and sometimes additional ancillary or volunteer help with transport, creches, camping and various specialist activities. It also requires staff who are willing and able to offer consultation and supervision to social workers undertaking groupwork.

Skill

Groupwork is a skilled activity and any agency which offers groupwork to clients needs to invest resources in groupwork skill development for staff. This may involve mounting in-service training programmes and funding staff to take relevant post-qualifying courses outside the agency. It may also mean paying external consultants, or appointing internal consultant staff to develop groupwork in the agency.

Accommodation

The impact of the physical environment on a group and its well-being has already been referred to. Unfortunately, for many practitioners, the question 'What are the best surroundings for this group?' is rather academic because they are struggling to find any accommodation at all. There are very few agencies that provide group rooms, so existing rooms have to be adapted from their primary purpose, or accommodation has to be sought in the community, and begged, borrowed or hired.

Accommodation considerations include the following:

(a) Physical requirements. How much space is needed? How many rooms? Can boisterous, messy, noisy activities be done? Is a carpet needed? Is there a kitchen or at least coffee-making facilities? Are toilets available? Is outside space needed?

(b) Geographical location. Is the place reasonably accessible to the members, and near to public transport routes?

(c) Venue. Is agency or neutral territory preferred?

(d) Cost. Is there a budget allowance for renting accommodation?

(e) Boundary protection. Whether agency or non-agency property, the accommodation is likely to be shared with other groups and used for other purposes. It is important to ensure that the group's time boundary is protected at both ends, and the physical boundary protected during sessions. This may be difficult when a group is located in a large residential establishment or in part of a large busy agency building, but interruption, whether innocent or 'sabotage', can be very disrupting.

(f) Using what you have. For example a social worker with an adolescent group had no alternative but to meet in a room that was used as a juvenile court. This was exploited by a very successful sociodrama session re-enacting a court scene.

Facilities and equipment

Groups vary in their requirements for equipment, from chairs or cushions for a discussion group, to workshops and sports equipment for some activity groups, to video equipment for social skills training groups. Groupworkers often have to work hard obtaining funds even for coffee and orange squash, never mind the more expensive items. Negotiating and advocacy skills are needed, short-term for obtaining the facilities for any one group, and long-term for influencing agency policy on groupwork equipment and funds. In some groups, members themselves can contribute or obtain resources, and this can be a way of sharing responsibility for the group.

Transport

Groups may need transport for two purposes. One is to get people to the group sessions, the other is for group activities, e.g. outdoor pursuits. The former is not just a question of resources, it also involves assessment of need and the desirability or otherwise of fostering dependency. Transport at the door can be an essential help to a mother with young children, whereas in other circumstances it can diminish personal responsibility and choice about whether or not to attend a group meeting.

Group composition, size, time and selection

When the need for a group has been identified, objectives clarified, and resources obtained, the next concerns are its composition, size and the selection of members and workers. Each of these will be considered in turn, drawing on theoretical guidelines where these are available, as well as practice experience. There are aspects of group composition on which theorists diverge, but there are also some guidelines which have general support (Hartford, 1971;

Yalom, 1975). The evidence on group size is more clear-cut because this is a single variable about which fairly confident predictions can be made. By contrast, not much has been written to guide selection criteria for the groupworkers themselves. (For general guidelines on co-worker selection see Hodge (1985), and for specific guidelines on black/white co-worker pairings see Mistry and Brown (1991).)

Group composition

The key decisions in group composition are concerned with homogeneity and heterogeneity, balance and compatibility. Redl's law of 'optimum distance' states that groups should be 'homogeneous enough to ensure stability, and hetero-geneous enough to ensure vitality' (1951). Homogeneity is needed to develop group cohesion, and heterogeneity is necessary to produce the forces for change in a group. The emphasis will depend on whether the aim of the group is primarily change, or support.

The need for balance requires that on any continuum of attributes, no individual is too far removed from at least one other, e.g. it is not generally a good idea to have one person who is twenty years older (or younger) than anyone else, or who is the only one of his or her sex, or who is the only person from a particular social class, ethnic group or culture. Every new group member has a need to feel compatibility (common identity, and/or complementary needs, and/or mutual liking) with at least one other member. If this initial link with another person is not present, it is likely that the 'singleton' member will feel herself to be, and often actually is, marginalised within the group process. This frequently leads to that person discontinuing membership of the group. If the singleton member is black, female, old or homosexual or has a disability, they are even more likely to be margina-lised and to drop out of the group.

A useful way of thinking about group composition is outlined by Bertcher and Maple (1977) in their manual *Creating Groups*. Drawing on research, they have developed an approach based on homogeneity of *descriptive attributes* and heterogeneity of *behavioural attributes*.

Descriptive attributes.   Descriptive attributes are factual descriptions of an individual e.g. woman, black, middle-aged, physically disabled, each of which carries associated role positions, status and stereotypes, which will have a profound influence on group interaction and that person's role in the group. Hare (1962) refers to research indicating that people with higher social status in the community who attend a group are likely to participate more and take more assertive roles (and conversely). This arises from role-expectations not only on their part but also from other group members who may defer to them because of their socially ascribed higher status.

This 'importing' of social attitudes into the group makes group composition of great significance for group process and task achievement. It means that groupworkers and potential members need to anticipate the likely consequences of particular types of group composition, and either seek to avoid unhelpful combinations or where this is not an option to make strenuous efforts in the group to compensate for potential marginalisation and stereotyping of individuals. (For a more comprehensive discussion of anti-discriminatory groupwork, particularly in relation to race and gender, see Chapter 6 in this book.)

Key descriptive attributes include the following:

(a)   *Age.* Most writers favour a limited age-range, especially for children's and adolescents' groups, bringing together people at a similar developmental stage. Variations on this are family groups where membership of the family system is the criterion, and those problem-focused groups where another descriptive attribute may be more significant than age, for example alcohol dependency.

(b)   *Gender.* Early studies of groups with mixed and same-sex composition drew some tentative conclusions about the ways in which sex balance can affect group process and outcome. They suggested, for instance, that there are advantages in single-sex groups for children and younger adolescents (Hartford, 1971). More recent studies of same-sex and mixed-sex groups have produced some interesting and important conclusions (see Reed and Garvin, 1983 and Davis and Proctor, 1989, for detailed reference to research findings and practice implications). There is evidence that all-female groups give more prominence to expressive issues of feelings and relationships than do their all-male counterparts, and conversely all-male groups are likely to be significantly more competitive and status-oriented. In mixed groups the females often 'accommodate' the men by facilitating their capacity to express personal feelings, without any equivalent gain for themselves. This is a generalisation and there are of course many mixed groups which are of equal benefit to both sexes: these tend to be those groups where at least half the members are women and where an ethos more akin to that in all-female groups prevails. The more that personal identity, empowerment and social role are central to the group task the stronger the case for a same-sex group, and conversely.

Women's groups have been well established in the last 20 years (see for example Ernst and Goodison, 1982; Hanmer and Statham, 1988; Krzowski and Land, 1988; and Butler and Wintram, 1991), and the particular need for them in male-dominated contexts such as the criminal justice system is gradually being recognised (see for example Mistry, 1989; and Jones *et al.*, 1991). Men's groups on the other hand have tended to exist for 'negative' reasons, by which I mean because there is no other choice as in all-male contexts such as a male prison. There is however a growing interest in men's groups created specifically to work in a personal way on issues arising from being male in a male-dominated society. These include groups focusing on issues of male identity, sexuality, power and violence. (The literature is quite sparse, but see Reed and Garvin, 1983; and McLeod and Pemberton, 1987.)

Gender is also an important factor in selection of the worker(s) for a group. Depending on the type of group, female workers in mixed groups tend to have a harder time than males because of perceived role incongruence causing group members to be more critical and testing (see Chapter 6 for more discussion of matching worker gender to different group compositions and tasks). Male–female co-worker pairings need to plan consciously for equality of responsibility and power because group members will tend to make assumptions of male dominance.

(c) *Race and ethnicity.* Many of the processes and principles outlined above in respect of gender also apply when considering race and group composition (see Davis and

Proctor, 1989). There are however at least two important differences. One is that whereas women comprise approximately half the population throughout the world, the proportion of 'non-white' people and the range of ethnic minorities varies greatly in different countries. In Britain, black people (when defined as including all who are 'non-white') comprise only 5 per cent of the population. This means that there is always a likelihood that a black person will find herself in a minority if not a singleton position in racially mixed groups. Davis (1980 and 1984) has developed the concept of the 'psychological majority' whereby people are *perceived* as being in the majority in a group if their representation significantly exceeds the expected 'norm'. Thus the white members of a group with equal numbers of black and white members can experience this as being in a minority.

The statistical probability of having just one or two black members in a mixed group poses a composition issue. In most circumstances this imbalance is very unsatisfactory because it puts a lot of pressure on the black person(s) who will find it difficult to be her/himself because of being viewed as 'the black member'. This reduces the likelihood of the group meeting that person's needs.

It is preferable therefore to have either an all-black group or a group with roughly equal black and white representation. The difficulty is that there may not appear to be sufficient black potential members for either of these alternatives. This issue requires a proactive anti-racist approach by the workers, in consultation with the potential black members, to create group conditions and external support systems which offer black members genuine equal opportunity in group programmes. One example of this is drawing membership from a wider catchment area than the single team or day centre, and having at least one black co-worker.

The second feature when considering race and group composition is ethnicity. If the main focus of the group is on racism, ethnic differences between non-white people may be less important then their common experience of having to combat racial discrimination. If on the other hand the focus is on a culture-related topic, say a reminiscence group for older people, fundamental cultural differences, including language, may get in the way of a mutually shared history.

Also people from different cultures have different 'rules' about group behaviour, for example on self-disclosure and the importance of 'saving face'. This raises further questions about the desirability and feasibility of ethnic-specific groups, and the practice issues in mixed-ethnicity groups. Turning to leadership, the black worker faces issues of perceived status and role incongruence which are similar to, but often starker than, those faced by female workers. The research indicates that groups are often less tolerant of shortcomings in the performance of a black worker than they are of exactly similar shortcomings in her white counterpart. This is of particular importance when it comes to selection of black/white co-workers, a subject discussed in detail by Mistry and Brown (1991). Davis (1980 and 1984) stresses the importance of white workers of racially mixed groups having a basic understanding of the impact black history, racism and environmental factors will have on group dynamics and process. Smith (1985) has also drawn together some of the British and US research on this subject.

(d) *Social class.* Once again, this time in respect of class, social discrimination in the wider society will be reflected in group behaviour, and therefore needs to be taken account of in group composition: if not in the actual decision about group membership then certainly in anticipating group process consequences to be counteracted. Davis and Proctor (1989) make the point that there is less literature on groupwork and class than on race or gender. They wonder if it is because much of the research is conducted with middle-class college students (and, I would add, by middle-class researchers!) What research there is suggests that people on low incomes may have a greater acceptance of class hetero-geneous groups, than do middle-income people, though this does not of course necessarily mean that their personal gain from a 'mixed class' group is not diminished by middle-class dominance. In task-focused structured groups class differ-ences may be less important than those in which customs and values are high on the agenda.

The same kind of group processes described in respect of the race, age and gender of the workers apply also in respect of social class. One point not previously emphasised is the boost having a worker of your own race, gender or class can be to the black, female or working-class group member respectively, particularly if that person models confidence and competence in the group for all to see, i.e. a good role model and support.

(e)   *Type of problem/life situation.* Some in this category are fairly clearly descriptive attributes, e.g. prisoner, lone father, parent of a child with a disability, sexually abused adolescent girl, non-attender at school, foster parent. Others are much more subjective descriptions and behaviourally labelled, e.g. depressed, delinquent, socially isolated.

Behavioural attributes.   These refer to the ways in which individuals actually behave (past and present), their personality, attitudes and life-styles. Behaviours are, of course, much influenced by context and by role-expectations associated with descriptive attributes, but for a given 'set', individuals do vary behaviourally on a range of continua, e.g. task orientation–relationship orientation, talkative–quiet, dominant–submissive, leader–follower, spontaneous–controlled, fighter–appeaser, initiator–reactor, patient–intolerant, introvert–extrovert. Any group concerned with change needs variety in the range of behaviours, skills and experiences which the members (and the workers) bring, combined with sufficient commonality of basic decriptive attributes.

Bertcher and Maple (1977) state that effective groups are those in which members are interactive (talk to each other freely); compatible (show that they like one another); and responsive (interested and active in helping and being helped). Barriers to effective groups include too much or too little compatibility; too much or too little stress; too few role-models; and negative sub-groups.

The following examples were drawn from a voluntary agency specialising in groupwork with lone parents:

Example: A short-life 'closed' discussion group was composed of separated and divorced mothers bringing up children on their own, and not employed. Both workers were also female. The homogeneity of descriptive attributes (female, white, separated or divorced, parent, non-working) was reinforced by behavioural homogeneity, in that all the women were feeling low and depressed in equal degree. There was an atmosphere of 'sameness', which, combined with a lack of initiators and extroverts, and no obvious work-leaders or role-models, created a group bereft of positive forces for change. The group struggled to develop at all, due to too much similarity, and too little tension (manifest actually in the group, as distinct from in individual members' private lives). The inclusion of some members emerging from their depression, a wider range of personalities, and workers more attuned to empowering feminist practice, might have created more favourable conditions for change.

Example: A short-life 'closed' discussion group was composed of widowed, separated and divorced fathers, bringing up children on their own, some employed and some unemployed. There was a mixed social class and cultural background, and male/female co-workers. This group was less descriptively homogeneous than the previous one, but the combination of basic descriptive similarity, i.e. fathers bringing up children alone, plus behavioural variations in personality and life-style, combined with two or three convincing and optimistic role-models, and a female co-worker, all seemed to provide a dynamic group composition and a more effective group (as rated by consumer feedback) than in the previous example.

These two groups were not evaluated in any systematic way but the apparently contrasting outcomes are consistent with both Redl's maxim and the Bertcher and Maple guidelines. An invaluable asset, which can sometimes be planned, is having one or two members in a group who take responsibility at an early stage (referred to by Shulman (1984) as 'internal leaders'), setting an example to others and enhancing group motivation and commitment.

'Stranger' versus 'acquainted' members. Finally, there is the important distinction between groups composed of strangers, and groups containing some or all members who already know each other and/or the worker. In natural groups, and groups in residential and day centre settings, people are already in some relationship with one another, and that is a given circumstance to be worked with. In field settings, there is the possibility of choice.

Having some members who are previously acquainted can be beneficial if those relationships are basically positive and open, lending the group stability and a growth point. Conversely, antagonistic or cliquey acquaintances can disrupt or unbalance a new group.

Members with previous or continuing individual relationships with the worker(s) can face difficulties, particularly when the worker is in some authority or assessment role, and issues of confidentiality arise. A group with only one member in that position is not recommended as it puts undue pressure on that individual. Two or more are in a stronger position. A group in which either none or all have known the worker previously is often not practicable: the important thing is that whenever possible 'imported' relationships are acknowledged early on in the life of the group because they will inevitably affect group process.

Group size

The information on group size available from small group research (Hartford, 1971) is firm enough to be useful for practitioners. If we assume the minimum size of a small group to be three members and the maximum about twelve the following factors are associated with increasing size in this range:

(*a*)   The number of one-to-one relationships increases rapidly, e.g. three pairs in a three-person group, fifteen in a six-person group, thirty-six in a nine-person group.

(*b*)   Sub-groupings are more likely (especially from eight members upwards).

(*c*)   'Physical freedom is restricted, while psychological freedom is increased' (Slater, 1958). In larger groups there is less space and time for each person, but more freedom to rest or be inconspicuous, and more opportunity to identify with other role-models. (In very small groups of three or four, individuals may be over-exposed and under-stimulated.)

(*d*)   Problem-solving takes longer, but may produce better solutions.

(*e*)   More specific roles tend to emerge, and be highlighted.

(*f*)   The very active and talkative members become more so, and conversely, the reticent become less likely to participate verbally (see Chapter 4 on programme for ways round this).

There is considerable agreement that a group size of five or six members (large enough for stimulation, small enough for participation and recognition) is the optimum for many purposes, particularly for the more therapeutic person-centred type of short-term closed group. For problem-solving, activity and 'open' groups, larger groups provide more resources and can work well. The tendency to sub-grouping can be used constructively by sub-dividing the group for various tasks and activities. Larger groups usually require more organisation and structure and may be more likely to need two workers, depending on the extent of leadership among members.

Social work groups often have a drop-out factor both at the stage of group formation (one or two expected members may never actually join the group) and during the group's life. There is also the inevitable temporary absence through illness or other indisposition. For all these reasons, it is desirable to aim for a membership two or three in excess of the required size. This applies particularly in 'closed' short-term groups where replacements may not be possible.

Time-scale

Decisions also need to be taken about the length, frequency and duration of sessions. It is not possible to generalise about these factors as decisions depend on the type of group and its purpose, and may often be negotiated with members anyway. In recent years the tendency in casework to favour brief task-focused intervention has to some extent been paralleled in groupwork with a shift in emphasis from groups that last for years, to ones that are much briefer in duration (say six to twelve sessions over a three- to six-month period), and specific in intent. Groups which *may* require longer time periods include some children's groups, therapy groups, natural groups, support and maintenance groups (e.g. for people suffering from chronic illness) and some groups in residential settings.

Meeting weekly has some advantages over fortnightly, both in keeping up the momentum and in facilitating attendance by a regular commitment in the week's arrangements. Flexibility in the use of time for different purposes is, however, essential, and some groups may be most effective meeting intensively over a short period, e.g. several times a week, a whole day, or over a block of three or four days. This intensive block or high frequency approach does not only apply to children's camps and sensitivity marathons, but has been found to be very effective with a whole range of other groups: for example in mental health crisis intervention; for perpetrators of child sexual abuse (Cowburn, 1990); and for specialist groups for other categories of offenders in the probation setting (Mackintosh, 1991). This level of commitment will not be practicable for many social workers with heavy workloads, but with careful planning and a flexible team approach, work patterns can be varied. For some workers and some members, a well planned block of a few days may be easier to cope with logistically than a weekly group over a three-month period. The cultural patterns and life-styles of the members are important considerations when deciding the timing of groups, particularly the time of day likely to be most acceptable and convenient, and the optimum length of sessions. See Alissi and Casper (1985) for a series of articles on 'Time as a factor in groupwork'.

Open groups

Open groups can be defined as those groups that have an open changing membership and often also an open-ended life-span. Until quite recently remarkably little attention has been given to this type of group. This is surprising because a study in the USA indicated that open groups are used very extensively there (Schopler and Galinsky, 1984; Galinsky and Schopler, 1985), and there is no reason to believe that the situation is any different in Britain or other European countries. Ziller (1965) indicated that the main disadvantages of a changing open membership are possible instability, precariousness and loss of leadership. He suggested the main advantages to be the potential creativity, flexibility and opportunities for changing a group's culture. A crude guideline is to think of closed membership as rather more likely for short-term groups, and planned open membership as more likely to be preferred long-term. Galinsky and Schopler analysed 66 open groups (1985) in their study and propose the following classification of open groups by group purpose:

    (i)   helping clients cope with transition and crises

(ii)   providing other types of short- and long-term therapy
(iii) offering support to clients with common problems
(iv)   assessing and screening clients
(v)   orienting and educating clients
(vi)   training and supervising staff and students
(vii) facilitating outreach efforts

One interesting point that emerges from their study is the frequency with which open groups are used for the first purpose listed above i.e. 'helping clients cope with transition and crises', the very process of joining and leaving an open group being useful experience in itself of coping with transitions.

Within the open concept there can be great variation, stretching along a continuum from groups whose membership changes very slowly (and whose characteristics therefore are quite similar to those of a closed group) to those which change continuously and barely merit the term 'group'. Michael Henry (1988) has developed a classification of three different models. These are *Drop-in (Drop-out)*, *Replacement* and *Re-Formed* groups:

Drop-in (Drop-out) groups are those which set few conditions on attendance or membership, other than any defined by the purpose of the group e.g. a women's drop-in group that any woman can attend. People can come and go as they please, so workers and members have no idea how many people or who will turn up each time. People who 'drop-out' of this type of group can re-enter when they wish, perhaps months or even years later. Some would say that these are not groups in the true sense of the word but more 'collectivities' (Lang, 1986; Brown and Clough, 1989; and Chapter 5 in this book). Be that as it may, 'drop-ins' make special demands on workers, who need to be versatile, informal, flexible and proactive in style. There are special skills involved in helping people to feel they belong without being committed, and in 'getting alongside' someone who may have a pressing need but is ambivalent and anxious about getting involved. There is also the potential problem, common to many open groups, of a few 'old' members tending to set the culture and climate of the drop-in, potentially deterring newcomers. Stones (1989) discusses a further issue in the context of a family centre which combines a drop-in with other more structured groups: many new members start off in the drop-in and then find it difficult to adapt to the greater structure and demands of other more organised groups in the centre.

Replacement groups are those with a fixed maximum size and controlled changes in membership as participants leave and are replaced by others. By controlled I mean that there is often a mechanism for joining and leaving involving other members and the workers in varying degree. Participants are more likely to make some sort of contract, or agreement (see later in this chapter) governing their length of stay in the group and criteria for exit. Galinsky and Schopler's research in the USA (1985) revealed that replacement groups often have clearly defined procedures/rituals for entry and exit: for example on entry, introduction exercises, statements of group purpose, and review of group history; and on exit, group evaluation of progress, leaving exercises, discussion of future plans and sometimes a social occasion with refreshments. There was variation in the extent to which these procedures were managed by the group members or the groupworkers: this variation will reflect the different models and styles of group.

Re-formed groups are a way of increasing the predictability of membership by the use of time boundaries (M. Henry, 1988). These groups meet for a set period of time, sometimes called a 'term', during which members may leave but no new ones join: members contract in for this agreed period. At the end of the fixed period, and usually after a break of a few weeks, a new re-formed group begins including some of the old and some new members (see Jones *et al.* (1991), for an example of this approach with women's groups in the probation setting). This approach attempts to combine the advantages of fixed membership with those of 'new blood'. One of the worker skills is enabling the new group to form in a way which both acknowledges what the old members have to offer from their experience, and is also genuinely open to integrating the new members and incorporating what they bring.

One of the big questions when thinking about open groups is whether the changing membership means constantly going back to the beginning each time. Sue Henry (no relation!) has an interesting section on open groups in her textbook (S. Henry, 1981) in which she suggests that many open groups exhibit a continuity of process even though the structure changes. By this she means that factors to do with group aims, history and tradition persist despite membership changes, thus providing a measure of continuing group development. Many readers will be members of work groups or teams which are an example of an open group with a persisting tradition and culture – which can of course be a mixed blessing!

Methods of group selection

The discussion so far has sidestepped the question of *who* makes the decisions about eligibility for, and actual membership of, a group. There is a range of possibilities, and clarity about the approach to be used will reduce possible ambiguity, muddle and resentment later.

(a)   Self-selected groups. These include spontaneously formed 'natural' groups, e.g. peer group in a neighbourhood.

(b)   Unrestricted membership groups. These include open groups which anyone can join if the aims interest them, e.g. a 'drop-in' centre.

(c)   Situationally determined groups. Here, eligibility is decided by descriptive criteria, e.g. being a resident of a hostel, the spouse of an alcoholic, living in a block of flats, being a lone father.

(d)   Group-selected. In some open groups the selection of new members is a matter for the group itself, once it is in existence.

(e)   Agency-selected (control by exclusion). In many groups the agency (management, team or groupworker) controls membership by deciding both the descriptive criteria, e.g. parents with children in care, adolescents with learning difficulties; and specific group composition and size, e.g. a closed group for adults with learning disabilities up to a maximum of ten.

(f)   Agency-selected (control by inclusion). In this model, group membership is compulsory and a requirement of some form of statutory supervision or care, e.g. a condition of probation or in-patient psychiatric treatment. Groupworkers and theorists (Roberts and Northen, 1976) differ on the ethics of compulsory group membership, but there is unanimity that the position should be explicit and stated clearly in the group contract.

Worker and co-worker selection

This aspect of group composition is often neglected in the literature and arrived at quite arbitrarily in practice. Perhaps it is too close for comfort! It will be considered in Chapter 3 on leadership, but is mentioned here as part of group composition because conscious and task-oriented choices of worker(s) need to be made at a very early stage in group preparation.

Prediction of group behaviour

As indicated earlier, some heterogeneity of behavioural attributes is needed in group composition, at least when the aim is some form of change. This requires the groupworker (if she is controlling group selection) to be able to predict how an individual will behave in a small group. Most social workers probably rely on a combination of hunch, previous information about a person (often second-hand from colleagues or records) and an individual interview. How reliable is such a prediction likely to be? Yalom's conclusion after surveying the available research literature is 'of all the prediction methods, the traditional intake individual interview appears the least accurate and yet the most commonly used.' That is not to deny the value of an individual interview as part of the group composition and contract-making stage, but to indicate its limitations as a predictor of group behaviour. Yalom continues '. . . An individual's group behaviour will vary depending on his internal psychological needs, his manner of expressing them, and the task, interpersonal composition and norms of his social environment.' He then states a general principle: '. . . the more similar the intake procedure is to the actual group situation, the more accurate will be the prediction of his behaviour' (Yalom, 1975).

This finding, with its self-evident simplicity, might suggest the value of obtaining information about any previous group experience, but this may be unreliable or non-existent. One approach is to set up some kind of intake or 'suck it and see' group, where in a few sessions, both worker and prospective member can obtain a much more accurate assessment of whether a group is likely to be the most helpful kind of intervention for that person at that particular time. This approach is already used quite extensively in the USA and in some groupwork programmes in Britain, e.g. intake/induction groups for new probationers (Brown and Seymour, 1983). An ingenious alternative, mooted by Yalom, is to show a simulated group situation, say a film or video-recording, to prospective group members and then invite them to share their reactions, feelings and identifications with the group and its members. If a film is not available, potential group members can be asked to write down and discuss their feelings about being with other people in groups, perhaps stimulated by suitable photographic images. Another option, well suited to open groups, is for a prospective member to attend for a few sessions to see how they get on: this can of course disrupt group cohesion so needs to be handled carefully.

Practical constraints on group composition

The reality of life in most social work agencies means that group composition is often influenced by factors beyond the individual social worker's control. This calls for a pragmatic approach, but the beginner is recommended to take into account the general guidelines suggested in this section and to resist pressures to take someone who seems quite unsuited to the group. The more experienced groupwork colleague will not necessarily pay less attention to group composition, but one of the skills that grows with experience is an ability to respond flexibly and creatively whatever the group and its composition, including acknowledging incompatibility when it arises.

Negotiating a contract

The notion of contract in social work

The contract or 'working agreement' approach to social work intervention is now widely used (see Preston-Shoot, 1989). It has two main advantages. One is a philosophy which acknowledges that users of services have a right to participate in decisions about their own 'treatment'. The other is a technique which attempts to be more clear and explicit about the aims and methods to be used, and the mutual obligations and expectations of all the participants, including the social worker. A potential disadvantage is inflexibility and unresponsiveness to changing needs. The contract may be written or verbal, the negotiating process itself having as much value as the content. Some literature tends to assume a bilateral worker/user(s) contract, but in statutory agencies a tripartite agency/worker/user concept is needed. The user and worker meet primarily because the agency has functions which it employs workers to carry out, and the user has needs or problems which the agency has a community-sanctioned responsibility to respond to. When several people are involved, as in groupwork and family therapy, individual contracts, e.g. regarding goals, have to be reconciled with group or family contracts.

A cardinal rule in contract-making is to be realistic and practical about the level of commitment and achievement which can reasonably be expected of each person.

The contract in groupwork

The main areas to be clarified are:

(a)   The aims of the group. What is the group for? (Avoid vague statements.)
(b)   Individual goals, consistent with the group aim. What does each individual hope to achieve through group membership?
(c)   The methods to be used. Members need to have a general idea of the methods to be used, e.g. discussion, role-play, games, and of any activities that are physically or emotionally demanding and whether participation in them is voluntary.
(d)   The practical arrangements of time and place and duration.
(e)   Rules, rewards and sanctions (if any), e.g. no violence in the group, early discharge of supervision, outings.
(f)   Individual commitments, e.g. to attend regularly, to work at individual goals, to help others.
(g)   Confidentiality. In what circumstances, if any, would the worker communicate information about a group member

to others in the agency or elsewhere? Is there a group agreement on confidentiality? Are group records or tapes to be accessible to members?

(*h*) Other social work service. What is the agreement about individual ex-group contact with social workers during the life of the group?

(*i*) Agency factors. For members: how does group participation affect any statutory relationship with the agency? For worker(s): what is the agreement with the agency on resources, workload recognition, supervision, insurance and other matters?

Contract negotiability

Different approaches to contract-making offer different levels of negotiating power to the members and worker(s) respectively. Three positions illustrate the continuum of worker–member power: low, medium and high negotiability.

Low negotiability implies a situation where the worker-power is high, and the member-power is low. The group-worker(s) make(s) all the major decisions about the group and the contract content, and the prospective member then decides whether or not to contract in to a largely predetermined package. In a coercive setting, he may be compelled to enter the group on the worker's terms.

Medium negotiability suggests rather more equality: worker-power and member-power may both be defined as 'medium'. The worker decides initially some broad outline goals and means, perhaps already influenced by ideas from prospective members. Participants then have the power to negotiate with her and other members about these and to modify and change them within defined limits, at initial contract-making meetings.

High negotiability implies that worker-power is low, and member-power is high. The worker does little more than provide the resources to enable a group to form and meet. The group membership makes all the major decisions about goals and *modus operandi*. The contract issues to be resolved in this model are mainly between members rather than between member and worker.

The degree of negotiability will vary according to the particular model and philosophy, the aims, the type of membership, the agency expectations and the individual social worker's style. Misunderstandings can arise when it is not clear how decisions are made and who makes them. The 'unforgivable sin' sometimes committed by groupworkers is to appear to be very democratic by inviting members' views on everything to do with the group's functioning, and then to exclude them from all the major decisions. When that happens, *actual* negotiability is much lower than *apparent* negotiability, and group members have every right to question the groupworker's credibility and integrity.

Contract negotiation stages

The following account of contract stages in formed groups is an elaborated version of that developed by Croxton (1974). The various terms themselves, e.g. 'preliminary contract', will not necessarily be used in practice, but they do represent important processes in the formation of a group in a social work agency. The sequence will vary according to the circumstances (see Fig. 2.1, opposite).

Having established the need for a group during the exploratory stage, the worker normally has to negotiate with her agency for support and resources before seeking a membership. This constitutes the *worker–agency contract*. A *draft plan* outlining aims, methods and resource needs will be circulated to relevant individuals as part of the negotiating process. The aim is to obtain agreement with the agency about what they will offer (e.g. consultation, accommodation, transport) and what they expect in return (e.g. general information about the group, effective help for users). A written agreement is more necessary when there is reason to doubt whether verbal promises will be honoured!

In interdisciplinary settings, such as child guidance clinics or hospitals, negotiations involve staff from other disciplines, e.g. nurses, doctors, psychologists, on whose sanction, if not approval, the viability of the group and the space it needs may depend.

The next stage is that of publicising the group and attracting a membership. This involves identifying a 'reservoir' of potential members. The basic proposals need to be on paper in the form of a written outline, indicating how firm or negotiable they are. Recruitment methods can range from newspaper advertisements through public posters, agency posters, a

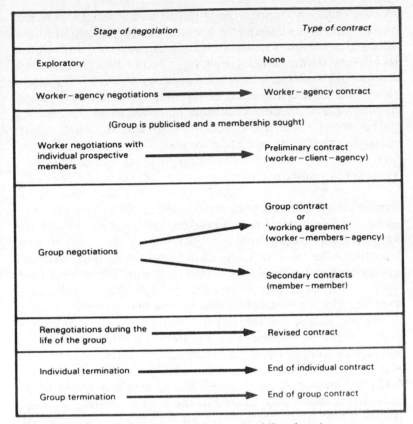

Stage of negotiation	Type of contract
Exploratory	None
Worker – agency negotiations $\longrightarrow$	Worker – agency contract
(Group is publicised and a membership sought)	
Worker negotiations with individual prospective members $\longrightarrow$	Preliminary contract (worker – client – agency)
Group negotiations	Group contract or 'working agreement' (worker – members – agency)
	Secondary contracts (member – member)
Renegotiations during the life of the group $\longrightarrow$	Revised contract
Individual termination $\longrightarrow$	End of individual contract
Group termination $\longrightarrow$	End of group contract

Note: Substitute 'working agreement' for 'contract' if preferred

Fig. 2.1

general letter or personal letters, to informal approaches and invitations. Recruitment may also be indirect via referrals from colleagues and other agencies. The more distant the source of referral, the more often it may be inappropriate, and special care needs to be taken in such cases (it is surprising what levels of 'misunderstanding' there can be even in referrals from close colleagues!)

Once a potential membership has been identified, the groupworker(s) will usually arrange a pre-group meeting with each prospective member to discuss their needs/problems and to discuss whether the group might have something beneficial to offer them. Joining a group can be a daunting prospect and

Manor (1986) suggests a three-stage process model in which the worker: first needs to *engage* with the individual and their personal concerns; then relates these to the group and what it may have to offer (*induction*); and finally has an exchange (*mediation*) about how the person's needs might, or might not, be met in the social context of a group of people with similar concerns and anxieties. This meeting provides an opportunity for questions to be asked about the group and what sort of things are likely to happen when it meets; for groupworker and prospective member to form an initial relationship, and for a mutual assessment to be made of the suitability of the person for the group and vice versa. Manor has followed up his theoretical framework with another article (1988) in which he gives a detailed practical example of the 'spiral process' of the pre-group meeting.

Both parties need to know what factors govern the decision to enter into a *preliminary contract* (e.g. does the worker have the power to exclude a prospective member?) even if this only commits the person to attending one or two group sessions in the first instance. Alternatively, more time and a further meeting may be needed. In some instances, significant others are included in the pre-group contract negotiations, for example, parents and teachers if it is a children's group.

Clients of statutory agencies are particularly likely to be ambivalent if not antipathetic to the idea of joining a group. Breton (1985) has contributed an important article on the subject, in which she rejects the notion of the 'unmotivated' person, and challenges groupworkers to understand the 'hard-to-reach' stance as having clear motivation based on concern about failure-avoidance, averting risks and maintaining control. If workers are to engage such people in groups they need, she says, to reach out on the other person's terms (and 'turf'), to demonstrate their own competence in practical ways, to offer challenges pitched at an appropriate level, and to involve natural support networks.

The next contract stage is that of group negotiations, leading to a primary contract or *working agreement*. Most groups start with a contract-making discussion. This is the point at which members can begin to shape the group programme. All the aspects listed above under the contract content need to be discussed, especially the link between individual and group goals. The worker outlines what the group may be able to offer members (emotionally or in activities or skill development) and explains his commitment and that of the agency. This stage can be time-consuming but is vital as a first experience of the worker's role and the decision-making process.

As a result of this negotiation, the prospective member either withdraws or makes a working agreement with the worker(s), the agency and other members. Specific undertakings between members, e.g. on confidentiality, are 'secondary contracts'. A written agreement should include any group rules and sanctions, and have separate sections outlining the respective undertakings of the group member, groupworker and the agency. Whilst a written agreement does not suit every group or everyone's style (and is the exception rather than the rule in current practice), it has the advantage over a verbal agreement that it is less open to misunderstanding and confusion. Its disadvantages can be formality, unhelpful pressure and inflexibility. Whether the agreement is written or not, provision needs to be made for contract review and renegotiation as part of a continuous process in which members take a greater share of responsibility for the group.

In closed, short-life groups, the group ends on an agreed date or when the group task is completed (or abandoned). Either way, contract termination at the group and individual level coincides. In an open group, the main criteria for ending an individual's group membership will be task completion as defined in the contract. The process of ending is considered in Chapter 4.

When a social worker negotiates with a natural group, she is an intruder into an existing social system. This makes it essential to define her role and the basis for her intervention, as well as the group members' undertakings to her and to each other. A preliminary contract, e.g. to discuss whether a basis for working together exists, is necessary to start this process.

Motivation and incentives

Many people are not naturally motivated to join groups unless there is some clear gain or benefit to be obtained, although once having joined a group, membership is often experienced as beneficial. An overall task of the groupworker at the preparation stage is to increase motivation by providing incentives and indicating potential gains from membership. It needs to be attractive. without being gimmicky. Equally, disincentives (e.g. when it is difficult or costly for someone to attend the group) are to be avoided. At the beginning of the life of a group, the worker's enthusiasm is seldom matched by that of the members; by the end it is frequently surpassed by theirs!

Groupwork planning exercise

The following checklist can be used both for training purposes and when preparing for a particular group:

(*1*)   The *need* to be met.
(*2*)   The *aim* of the group.
(*3*)   The *potential membership*? Who is it for? Who decides on recruitment/referral? Group size? Group composition? Will the group be advertised? If so, how?
(*4*)   The *leadership arrangements*? Who? How many? What roles?
(*5*)   Any particular *theoretical* or *philosophical* basis?
(*6*)   *Methods/techniques* to be used (and how far group programme is decided in advance).
(*7*)   *Group structure* e.g. open/closed, frequency, timing, and length of sessions/activities.
(*8*)   *Resources* needed, e.g. time, accommodation, materials, transport, finance.
(*9*)   Arrangements for *recording, evaluation, consultation/ supervision.*
(*10*) Do I need anyone's *permission* to start this group?
(*11*) Who do I need to *negotiate* with about this group, e.g. colleagues, managers, potential members, members' relatives, other agencies?
(*12*) What *obstacles* (to starting a group) are anticipated?
(*13*) What steps/strategies are necessary to overcome the obstacles and create the conditions for establishing the group?

Hodge (1977) has produced a more detailed planning outline in his article 'Social Groupwork: rules for establishing the group'.

3 Leadership in Groups (Including Co-working)*

Basic concepts

Leader and *leadership* are two terms that are frequently confused because they are defined and used in many different ways. *Leadership* is a *function* and according to Shaw's definition (1976) is 'a process in which one group member exerts positive influence over other group members'. 'Positive' is used by Shaw in the individual-centred sense of leading the group in the direction that group member chooses, which may not necessarily be towards the group goals. The term leadership will be used here, however, to mean influence which is positive in a group-centred sense, i.e. which helps the group to work at its task, achieve its goals, maintain itself in good working order and adapt to its environment. Leadership may be displayed by any member of a group at any time during the group's life. One way of using the term *leader* is to refer to any group member who is exercising leadership. *Leader* is also often used in the special sense of the person or persons who have a *designated* leadership role, e.g. chairperson, director, consultant, warden, groupworker, facilitator. The term 'worker' is sometimes used interchangeably with 'leader' in this context.

In most formed groups in social work, the social worker

* For this third edition I considered changing the title from 'Leaders and Leadership' to something like 'The role of the worker', thus substituting 'worker' for 'leader', partly because there has been some switch in general usage in this direction in recent years, probably reflecting a change in ideological emphasis. I decided to drop the term 'leader' from the title but to retain 'leadership' because, as explained above, leadership is a function needed in all groups and carried out by all members. 'Worker' is used to refer to the agency employee or associate who has a defined role which differentiates him or her from other group members. The 'worker' is not necessarily 'leader', but when reference is being made to the person in the designated role the latter term will sometimes be used.

has some kind of designated leadership role, at least in the early stages. She is seen and behaves as the 'central person' in the group, often being the person who formed the group and to whom more communications are made than anyone else. As the group develops, she may or may not continue to exercise the most leadership. In some models she will gradually move out of the central person role to a position where much of the group leadership is carried by the members. This possibility is often forgotten by anxious group leaders who feel they must carry all the leadership themselves, in the process denying members their potency. Natural groups, like the family or the gang, already have their own leadership structure, and one of the most difficult tasks for the social worker in that context is to establish a viable leadership role for herself which does not undermine the existing structure of the group or the position of the person or persons who are regarded as leaders.

Several theories of leadership are referred to in the literature. The first is the *trait* theory, which assumes that 'leaders are born and not made'. It is now largely discredited as unsupported by research, except for some rather old evidence (Stodgill, 1948) that group leaders do tend to show rather more general ability, sociability and motivation than group members.

The second is the *position* theory of leadership, in which leadership is defined by the formal role or position which an individual holds in an organisation or group.

The third is the notion of leadership as a *style*. The well-known study by Lippitt and White (1953) observed the effects of different leadership styles on activity groups of ten-year-old boys. The three styles, autocratic, democratic and *laissez-faire*, were compared. The principal findings, which have been validated by subsequent studies, indicate that the autocratic approach is at least as effective in task achievement and productivity as the democratic approach, but produces more dependence and resentment; the democratic approach is much more acceptable, satisfying and creative for the members; and the *laissez-faire* groups are less productive than the others, spending much time discussing their tasks. A simplistic conclusion that a democratic leadership style is always preferable has been superseded by a recognition that it all depends on the particular *situation* and *function* of the group. Interestingly, Shaw's research (1976) indicates that it is easier (though less acceptable to the members) to be an autocratic leader issuing orders, than a democratic leader utilising the abilities of group members effectively.

The fourth theory, developed by Fiedler (1967), is known as the *contingency* model of leadership, linking leadership styles to situational variables. He has shown that when the situation is highly favourable or unfavourable to the leader, a task-oriented style is most effective, but that when it is only moderately favourable, a more relationship-oriented style is required. Highly favourable means high position power, clear goals and methods and good leader–member personal relations. Fiedler's model provides a framework for matching leadership styles and behaviour to the needs of different situations.

Group leadership is concerned with two basic types of leadership, *task leadership* and *group maintenance leadership* (sometimes referred to as instrumental and expressive respectively). *Task-leadership* functions are directly concerned with task achievement and group goals, and include giving information and opinions, seeking information and opinions, initiating, giving directions, summarising, coordinating, diagnosing, energising, reality testing and evaluation. *Maintenance-leadership* functions are directed toward the feelings, relationships and participation of the people in the group and include encouraging participation, harmonising and compromising, tension-relieving, helping communication, evaluating the emotional climate, observing processes, setting standards, listening actively, energising, building trust and resolving interpersonal conflict. (These functions, which are based on extensive analysis of how people actually behave in groups, are discussed in more detail in Johnson and Johnson, 1975.)

An effective group requires both types of leadership. Studies show that most individuals tend to be either more task-oriented or more relationship-oriented in their natural style, though some have an even balance between the two. There are some quite simple paper-and-pencil tests (Johnson and Johnson, 1975, Appendix A) for rating your position on a leadership grid. Fig. 3.1 indicates four extreme positions.

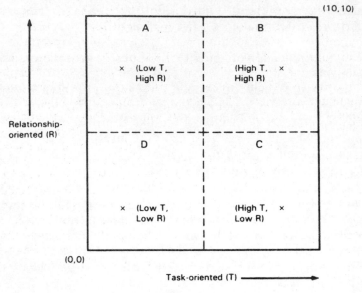

Fig. 3.1

A is a relationship-oriented leader, C is a task-oriented leader, B is high on both types of leadership, D is low on both types of leadership. There is no optimum position on the grid, because it depends on the type of group and the predominant need. Reddin (1970) suggests a third dimension of effectiveness, which is offering the appropriate leadership style when it is most needed in the group. This raises interesting questions about the leadership skills repertoire and flexibility of each individual. Some research (Lieberman, Yalom and Miles, 1973; Brown, 1977) suggests that most individuals actually range less widely in their leadership behaviour in different situations than they think they do. Palmer's research with probation officers in California (1973) indicates that with experience and further training, the social worker can develop new skills and extend his repertoire of behaviour, within certain limits. In casework, limits imply some matching of workers, clients and tasks, but in groupwork there is more flexibility because co-workers can offer complementary styles, as can group members. Most groups need both task and relationship skills, and if the worker has a bias this can be compensated for by a co-worker or members. (This whole subject of worker-repertoire in groupwork merits further study.)

Example: A social skills group for psychiatric out-patients. The designated leader is leading a role-play on interview technique. He is trying to help one member, Mike, to assert himself in a simulated interview. The leader first demonstrates how to do it himself, and then repeatedly gets Mike to rehearse the behaviour, but little change results. Suddenly, another member, Peter, calls out to Mike, 'Hey, Mike, what's up, you don't seem yourself today?' Mike bursts into tears and tells the group that his friend was killed in a road accident a few days previously. The group members commiserate with him, and the leader suggests he takes a rest while someone else takes a turn at being interviewed. A sensitive groupworker might himself have responded to the 'feel' of Mike, but the important thing was that one of the members did so, in the process exercising expressive leadership which enabled Mike to get support, and the group to get on with its task.

Authority, power and control

Much that happens in groups revolves around issues of authority, power and control. Social workers in statutory agencies have certain formal authority which derives from their role, professional authority which stems from their training and skill, and personal authority which emanates from their personality. This authority is associated with different kinds of power, classified by French and Raven (1967) as *legitimate* (vested in the role), *attraction* (power from being liked), *coercive* (power to punish), *reward* (power to reward) and *expert* (power of perceived expertise). The designated leader is able to exercise a degree of control over the members because they validate the authority and power which actually may be quite tenuous. Group members themselves also carry certain kinds of authority and power, and a potential for controlling the worker, other members and the group as a whole. The exercise of power and control may take various forms. Obvious examples are the worker who tells the group what to do and the member who dominates and tries to take over. Less obvious, but equally potent, is the worker who subtly manipulates the group in the direction he wants, or the member who takes a scapegoat role which preoccupies the rest of the group. Two anxieties often expressed by social workers leading groups are, paradoxically, discomfort about their authority and fear of losing control. Group members are not helped if the groupworker 'denies' her authority by behaving exactly as if she was one of them, and not in a different role. There is sameness in person encountering person, but difference in roles and responsibilities. If the worker has not come to terms with her own power and authority, she is unlikely to be able to help the members discover and use theirs. The skill lies in functioning as a complete person in a defined role. Authority figures attract other people's projections and strong feelings, which is what makes the acceptance of authority so uncomfortable at times.

The fear of losing control surges up in most groupworkers from time to time. What if the group members will not accept what I propose to do? What if there's a dominant person whom I can't control? What if there's total silence? What if two people start fighting? What if I 'fancy' one of the group members? And most unnerving of all, what if the group members make it clear that they think the group would do better without me? Most of these fears arise from the false premise that the group belongs to the designated leader, and she is responsible for all the controlling. Control systems in which the members carry power are likely to be more effective than those which are imposed on them.

Example: A group for people who find it difficult to express their feelings and emotions; with the goal of improving personal relationships. The two workers decided on a programme which would involve focusing each week on some particular feeling selected by the members, and approaching it by starting off with some experiential exercises linked to the theme, followed by group discussion. The members had accepted this format as part of the initial contract, and followed it with some reluctance for the first four sessions. Then at the beginning of the fifth session one of the members challenged the workers, saying he didn't see any point in doing 'the stupid exercises'. All the members remained silently rooted to their seats, giving passive support. The workers experienced their own anxiety and anger – their plan was being challenged, the whole thing was about to get out of control! After a very tense few minutes, negotiation started, and the planned format was abandoned on the under-standing that the members would take their share of respons-ibility for future planning and process. From that session onwards the group moved forward. A high level of commitment was reflected in one hundred per cent attendance at meetings and a sharing of responsibility for caring, controlling and working at the task. The group was now meeting the members' needs, within the contract, instead of the workers' preplanned ideas. The workers still had important roles and carried author-ity in the group, but based on legitimate, expert and attraction power, not coercive and reward power.

Lang (1972) has devised a continuum to indicate the different ways in which group control may be shared between leader(s) and members.

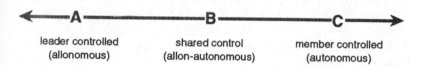

| leader controlled | shared control | member controlled |
| (allonomous) | (allon-autonomous) | (autonomous) |

This continuum can be used in two ways: firstly to locate the predominant position of a particular group model, and secondly to indicate movement in the balance of control during the life of a group. For example in 'remedial' models (Papell and Rothman, 1966) and many group psycho-therapies the worker retains a central 'allonomous' position A throughout, in complete contrast to self-help models which are autonomous right from the beginning, position C.

In mainstream social groupwork, the worker is often fairly active and directive at the beginning of a new group, functioning initially as the *central person*, position A, when group patterns are being established, central issues being sorted out, aims agreed and programme negotiated. But then as the group develops and members take on more responsibility, there is a decisive shift to the right and a position of shared control and responsibility, as in position B. What happens next in the latter stages of a fixed-life group depends on the particular model. If the goal is for members to assume responsibility gradually for their own group, then the movement will continue towards the autonomous position (B→C), whereas if the worker retains overall responsibility there is likely to be a looping back (B→A) as the worker again assumes a more central position to enable her to facilitate the group ending and all that entails.

The discussion so far may appear to have suggested that the 'leader(s)' have full control over what kind of role they take in these various models of responsibility-sharing with the group members. This is not the case because groups are dynamic and interactive and the members are continuously influencing the workers as well as vice versa. Heap (1988) has made an interesting observation on this issue in an article called 'The worker and the group process: a dilemma revisited'. He identifies two components in the central person role, the 'situational' and the 'emotional'. The 'situational' refers to the more obvious centrality which derives from being a professional staff member in an agency. This probably means that the worker has planned the group, controls certain resources and has taken various initiatives which place her in a key instrumental role at the outset. The 'emotional' refers to the expressive role experienced when the members relate to the worker in an emotionally dependent way to meet their own needs, perhaps of insecurity. Heap goes on to suggest that whereas the worker should and usually does shed the situational centrality as the group members take on responsibility for their group, she may not be able to shed her emotional centrality if the members wish to preserve her in that position psychologically. Some would argue that a worker's unconscious if not conscious needs may be feeding into this phenomenon which can be a block to member empowerment. The essential point being made here however is that the worker is rarely in full control of the position she attempts to take in the group.

Choice of worker

The means by which a groupworker is 'selected', a decision is reached to have either one or two workers, and a co-working pair is chosen, is often rather mysterious. Much less attention is given sometimes to worker selection than member selection, with far-reaching consequences for the group. At best, a rational decision is made to select one or more workers on the basis of the particular skills and attributes required to meet the group's needs and aims. At worst, an *ad hoc* decision emerges reflecting the personal and political interests of staff and/or agency management, paying scant attention to group interests. Scarcity of resources often means that the availability of staff becomes the deciding factor.

Example: A Family Clinic was planning to run a group for mothers, with a linked group for their pre-school children. A newly qualified social worker was keen to establish the group and did most of the preparatory work. It was decided that she and a senior social worker (male) would co-work with the mothers' group, and a child psychologist and health visitor would co-work with the children's group. The clinic was anxious to develop collaboration with health visitor colleagues in this way. Only a week before the group was due to start, the health visitors felt they would like to be directly involved with the mothers' group, and a decision was taken to switch the senior social worker and health visitor so the latter would team up with the newly qualified social worker as co-worker of the mothers' group, and the former with the psychologist taking the children. One consequence of this was that the two least experienced workers were working with the mothers, and another was that two female co-workers were working with an all-female group, who subsequently proved to be particularly preoccupied with their relations with men! This example illustrates in rather an extreme way how agency (and inter-agency) factors can influence worker-selection decisions.

Choice of co-workers is a crucial decision which can determine whether or not a group is successful, and the factors involved are considered in some detail in the following section on co-working.

Co-working

Co-working has become an integral part of social groupwork practice in Britain (see Brown, Caddick, *et al.* 1982) to the extent that the single-worker model now tends to be the exception rather than the rule. The reasons for this trend are not altogether clear, but appear to be associated with the struggle to get groupwork established in some agencies, and the perceived benefits of shared working, thinking and support in carrying out what is quite a complex task. The choice of a single or co-worker model has to be made at an early stage of planning a new group. As co-working is twice as expensive in staff resources (unless the second worker is a volunteer or student), good reasons are needed for having two workers rather than one, and it is necessary to demonstrate that there are increased benefits for the group members as well as for the workers themselves.

Potential benefits of co-working – for group members

Most of the potential benefits for group members arise from having two workers with distinctive characteristics who, in combination, can offer the group and each individual member more than either would be able to alone. These differences may include:

(a)   *basic characteristics*: age, gender, race, class. For example, mixed-sex groups and racially mixed groups may benefit from having male/female and black/white co-worker pairings respectively.

(b)   *role-difference*: e.g. field social worker/residential worker pairings; social worker pairings with health visitor, youth worker, prison officer, teacher, student, volunteer.

(c)   *personality/style difference*: e.g. sense of humour, assertiveness, openness.

(d)   *differences in prevailing mode of communication*: e.g. auditory, visual, kinaesthetic (feelings mode).

(e)   *knowledge/ideas/life experience differences*: each worker may bring specialist knowledge and understanding, and will have different life experiences. For example, it can be particularly helpful to group members if at least one of the co-workers shares a similar background experience or current condition, as for example in the group for people with Aids described by Getzel and Mahony (1989).

(f)   *differences in group skills*: e.g. one worker may be stronger on group task and the other on group maintenance; one on group activities, the other on group discussion; one more comfortable than the other with self-disclosure in the group.

(g) *worker–member ratio*: in larger groups, say eight or more, two workers can ensure adequate individual attention for each member, although this may not necessarily be regarded always by the individual as a bonus!

All these differences offer more choice and resources to the individual member when seeking what he needs, and also an increased chance of finding a worker with whom he feels particular rapport. It should not of course be forgotten that many of these varied attributes and resources will be in the group membership – one of the crucial differences from casework – and therefore are not necessarily an argument for having two workers.

The co-workers, as a pair, also offer a model of a relationship. The way they relate to each other, for example in managing disagreement, intimacy, conflict, crisis, caring, action, sharing feelings, offering support and so on can provide a helpful model for the members. Conversely if there are major tensions between them in some of these areas this can be an unhelpful if not destructive experience for the group. There are particular issues for both workers and members in certain kinds of pairings, for example male/female and black/white, and these will be discussed in more detail below.

Potential benefits of co-working – for the co-workers

There are several types of potential gain for the workers:

(a) *support*: both in the group, and outside the group in negotiations with colleagues, managers, resource-holders and so on.

(b) *professional development*: working with a colleague offers special learning opportunities through shared experience, mutual observation and giving and receiving feedback on each other's work performance. The 'apprenticeship model' of student and teacher co-working is a special example of this, although it can turn into a liability if the 'novice' is overwhelmed by the 'expert'.

(c)   *administrative benefits*: e.g. sharing tasks such as negotiating agency support, obtaining resources, writing letters and records, meeting prospective group members; and most importantly in longer-term groups, providing continuity when one member is ill or away on holiday.

(d)   *management and control*: in groups needing active management and control, as for example in some larger groups for young children or adolescents, a second or even a third pair of hands and eyes may be a necessity!

These 'worker benefits' do not necessarily in themselves justify co-working (the group is created after all for the benefit of the members!), but if they do enhance the quality and usefulness of the group for the members, in addition to any worker benefits, then they strengthen the case for committing the additional resource of having two workers. Conversely if the main, perhaps unconscious, aim is to protect the workers from stress and exposure, then co-working may not be in the members' best interests. There is quite a strong body of opinion in the USA that co-working can be counterproductive, and in particular that everyone training to be a groupworker should have some experience working with groups on their own to get the feel of being in a position of having to experience the full worker responsibility and group dynamic. Although I am convinced co-working can often be a very rich and productive approach to groupwork, single-worker experience was certainly an important part of my own training and one which I think all groupworkers need to experience at an early stage of their career.

Another factor to be considered is *worker-preference*. Some people are much more comfortable working in a pair than alone, others find the sharing irksome and an unnecessary complication. These preferences are important ones for the worker to recognise and 'own' because they may distort one's judgement about what is likely to be in the best interests of the group members. An example of an unhelpful kind of worker pairing is one in which the workers join together to indulge their own relationship. Any co-worker pair is a sub-group within the group, and it is important that this sub-group is open to the group rather than turned in on itself as sometimes happens.

In summary it is generally, but by no means always, true that the larger, more complex and problematic a group is, the stronger the case for two workers. Conversely, the small relatively straightforward group with highly motivated members willing and able to take responsibility may be best served by a single worker, if indeed one is needed at all!

Three-person or multiple leadership models are often fraught with difficulties arising from confusion about the roles and structure within the staff sub-group. This model should only be used when there is an overriding need for three or more workers, and when the roles can be clearly defined. An example of this would be an Intermediate Treatment group of, say, fifteen children, often engaged in activities in several sub-groups, and requiring a 5 : 1 ratio for adequate care and control. There might be one overall leader and two other workers with clearly distinguished roles.

The skills of co-working

Before outlining general leadership skills we shall consider skills specific to co-working. Most British textbooks (e.g. Preston-Shoot, 1987, Chaps 4 and 5) have major sections on this topic, and Hodge's practice guide *Planning for Co-Leadership* (1985) provides clear and comprehensive guidance. However, the current literature gives very little attention to issues of gender and particularly race factors in co-working (but see Mistry and Brown, 1991), and for that reason they are given prominent attention in what follows. The skills of co-working are considered here in two sections: *pre-group preparation* and *in-group skills*, the latter also including *work together outside the group* after it has started.

Pre-group preparation. The first stage is *the decision to work together*. Sometimes it is not even a decision, it just happens. This may be because there was no choice or because two people just assumed that they would work together. There are both negative and positive factors which contribute to what we have already seen can be a decision of great importance for the potential 'success' of the group. The choice of who works with who may not be an easy thing to talk about particularly in a team where there are choices and people have preferences about pairings, with the corollary of exclusions and less preferred colleagues. Even a firm emphasis that the decision is a professional one and not about personal likes and dislikes cannot remove the strong feelings which may be aroused. This statement is based partly on my own experience as a consultant working with teams on co-working, and trying to enable team members to express openly their feelings about working with different colleagues and with the team leader.

The decision to work together is always significant, but it is likely to be much more so in unstructured groups where much depends on process, and the workers are more exposed personally. In 'free-flowing' groups they will frequently be responding to the unexpected, by contrast with the greater predictability of structured group 'packages' of a more educational type in which the workers are implementing a predetermined albeit participative programme. This is highly relevant when considering race and gender factors in co-working. In the give-and-take of an unstructured group, issues of power, prejudice, discrimination and personal values are much more likely to come into prominence (see Mistry and Brown, 1991) and the values and attitudes of the co-workers to be exposed and tested, than in the 'safer' parameters of a predetermined programme.

Choice of pairing should be made as early as possible to avoid the situation which often occurs of one person being centrally involved from the beginning – perhaps the idea to have the group was theirs – and the co-worker being asked to 'join' at a late stage when many of the key decisions have already been taken by the other worker. In these circumstances it is very difficult to establish a genuine feeling that the groupwork and the overall responsibility are shared on an equal basis. Circumstances often dictate a less than ideal arrangement with one co-worker getting involved at a later stage than the other, and when this happens it is very important that the 'lop-sidedness' is recognised and the co-workers decide together how they are going to manage it.

They may decide to accept it as given and work on a primary/secondary co-worker model or they may decide to make strenuous efforts to redress the balance to a co-equals model, by for example the latecomer taking over major responsibilities.

Fundamental attributes like age, gender, disability and race, often get played down in the choice of co-worker and omitted from their discussions of the co-worker relationship. Yet we know from research (see Chap. 6 in this book) that these fundamental characteristics of the workers will have a profound effect on the members, who are likely to bring to the group stereotypical assumptions about for example who holds the power in male/female and black/white relationships. In addition to the impact on the members, both co-workers are likely to have strong feelings about whether their partner is of the same or a different age, sex and ethnicity which will affect how they work together, particularly if these feelings are not voiced. If one worker has a physical disability this may be even less likely to be mentioned. Competence, values, skills and 'personality' are of course also of primary importance, and in my view it is essential not to get into a polarised position of believing either competence or personal identity is all-important. It is the integration of the two which counts.

When two workers are exploring whether to work together, an exchange about personal *values* will probably be the most important of all. If for example one worker takes a very individualised view of groupwork and the other works from a social action perspective this may be a contraindication for co-working. Similarly if one of them has anti-discrimination at the top of her agenda and the other regards this as relatively unimportant compared to the task of the group they could be in trouble. Similarly if one views group process as paramount and the other is preoccupied with task and outcome, it may be difficult to plan the group together, although potentially their strengths are complementary provided they are mutually respected.

It is also important to explore those values issues that are likely to be particularly important for the prospective group (as distinct from groups in general). For example to go into a group where racism is likely to be central without having some shared view on whether it should be confronted, or into a group concerned with child sexual abuse without a shared view on the position of the non-abusing parent will at best be very confusing for the members, and at worst be positively destructive. I am not suggesting that co-workers should hold identical values or views – far from it – but that compatibility of values is essential particularly in groups where values are likely to be of central importance.

Many social workers find it difficult to articulate any specific *theoretical framework* which underpins their practice, but all have some theoretical assumptions which influence how they work. For example some groupworkers emphasise here-and-now relationships (humanistic psychology) and others hone in on behaviour as the key factor (learning theory). These frameworks for understanding need to be shared at this co-worker 'matching' stage.

There is no better way of testing out working together before reaching a final decision than actually doing it. This can be experienced through exercises and/or undertaking joint tasks. The 'draw-a-house' exercise is good fun and can be very revealing. The couple have to draw their 'dream-house' jointly holding one pen and without speaking. This gives them an experience of both sharing control – a key issue in co-working – and combining values/interests. It can get quite lively as on one occasion when one person drew a large cat lying on the lawn and their partner who hated cats immediately obliterated it with the pen without so much as some non-verbal consultation! Another exercise is 'following hands'. You stand facing one another and initially take turns in making arm movements which the other person mirrors. Then it is a free-for-all with each partner being both follower and leader as the spirit takes them. This is a good way of checking out deference, control and negotiation. The non-verbal aspect is important because frequently in a group the co-workers have to communicate feelings and responses to each other without speaking. Another more direct exercise is sharing feelings about co-working in general and about working with your prospective partner in particular. Each partner can be asked to state what their 'bottom-line' is for what they will expect from their co-worker. This might range from taking their fair share of the work to being able to confront sexism and racism to being sensitive to the need to give support at times of vulnerability.

The other way to test things out is to seek opportunities to work together on a joint basis perhaps in a training group or with a relatively straightforward social work task or team project. Some preliminary discussion of how the group might be run is another good way of checking to what extent approaches are compatible.

The second stage, having settled on a partnership, is *preparing to work together*. Just as groupwork itself involves task and relationship elements, so does the co-worker partnership in the pre-group phase. There is some work to do specifically on the relationship, and some to fulfil the preparatory tasks as outlined in Chapter 2. Involving a third person in a consultancy role is a good way of opening up communication about the more difficult relationship issues. Anxieties and fantasies can be shared and explored. For example, what are you feeling about the fact that your partner is black/white and you are white/black; that you are twenty years younger/older; that you are working with the opposite/same sex; that you are much more/less experienced than your partner; that s/he is your boss or practice-teacher; that you are feeling very apprehensive about the level of psychiatric disturbance of the group members and you are relying desperately on your partner to cope if things seem to get out of hand?

On the task side you need to decide who is going to do what, how you are going to co-ordinate different aspects of preparation and what you are going to do together. For example: who is going to sound out the team-manager for resources?; are the prospective group members going to be contacted jointly or separately?; what kind of records if any are going to be kept and which of you is responsible?; who arranges accommodation, transport and refreshments?; who contacts the potential consultant? If you were on your own you would at least know that everything to be done would be done by yourself even if you did have nearly twice as much work to do! Then there is planning the first meeting. Which of you is going to take on which responsibilities in the group, how are you going to split task and relationship responsibilities, and do you agree about how much to prepare/determine in advance and how much to leave for the group members to decide?

In-group skills. After all the preparation, planning and anticipatory anxiety the moment comes when the group actually starts and co-working together in the group begins. It is absolutely essential that the co-workers go into that first meeting having clarified together the plans for the session and how they will share the different elements of the programme. One very simple example is who is going to start and end the group session? Inexperienced workers working together for the first time will understandably probably overplan the first meeting and define their respective roles quite rigidly. Couples used to working together will have less need to 'insure' in this way against unfilled space and role confusion, but they too need to be very clear about their plans for the meeting and how they are going to work together.

Key issues at the beginning stage are likely to be time-boundaries, groundrules, programme negotiability, establishing group cohesion and behaving in ways congruent with the groupwork model to be adopted. Within the time set aside for reviewing the first meeting together, with or without a consultant/supervisor, should be space for explicit discussion of the co-working relationship. Did you feel supported by your partner, did each of you take your fair share of responsibility, did you get at cross purposes with each other, did the black co-worker experience his white colleague leaving the 'racism bit' to him to deal with, and so on?

Co-working means sharing the responsibility for work in the group fairly evenly, with neither partner consistently dominating or deferring to the other. There needs to be a sensitivity to what your colleague is feeling, experiencing and thinking, and an ability to support but not to over-protect when facing difficulties. Competitiveness and 'splitting' (sometimes provoked by group members) and any wish to appear more able than your colleague are to be avoided as they can only be unhelpful modelling for the group, if not actually destructive. A willingness to disagree with, or at least to question, your partner in the open group if you sense that what she is doing is not in the group's best interests, can be an asset provided it can be done in a facilitative and not an undermining style. Non-verbal skills like use of eye contact (facilitated by sitting opposite each other) are vital components of the in-group relationship.

One of the crucial skills of co-working is *responding to the unpredictable happening in the group*. A sudden crisis may occur with someone rushing out, being violent or crying hysterically. Some planned activity may not work or may develop differently from what was expected. In these circumstances, decisions have to be taken 'live' and any consultation can only take place publicly in the group, unless taking 'time-out' is incorporated by the co-workers in the model used. Much will hinge on the level of trust and mutual confidence between the two workers. In a well-developed group the members will naturally play a full part in the action and decisions, in a spirit of collective responsibility, and useful learning can result.

For all but the most experienced co-workers it will be essential to build in regular review and planning sessions between group meetings. This means allocating more time and should be included in any resource negotiations with managers and team-colleagues. As well as discussing the co-working relationship and group issues, the co-workers are in the invaluable position of observing each other's work first hand, and with a degree of trust this can be fed back to their partner. For example, most groupworkers respond differently to different group members, not just objectively by empathetic sensitivity but subjectively because of often unconscious personal resonations evoked by particular group members. In other words we sometimes 'hook-in' psychologically to another person. A colleague can point this out gently(!) enabling adjustments to be made.

In black/white co-working all the general skills and factors apply, but there are also special features linked to race and racism. In a recent article on black/white co-working (Mistry and Brown, 1991) some of these are identified and practice guidelines suggested. A point not emphasised sufficiently so far here, but one stressed in the above article, is the significance of the group members' expectations of, and reactions to, features of the co-working relationship, and the pressure this can put on the co-workers. This applies particularly to black/white and male/female pairings, when the members will tend to have stereotypical assumptions about roles and who holds the power. For example they may

expect male co-workers to be senior to their female counterparts. They may feel uncomfortable or threatened by a
black/white pair who work well and closely together, and
perhaps unconsciously seek to undermine their co-working
relationship. In a group with an all-white membership the
black co-worker often comes under enormous pressure
because of the covert if not overt group racism with which
her white colleague may have unwittingly colluded. This is
further exacerbated when the white co-worker leaves it to
his black colleague to pick up racist issues and do the
confronting. In this type of situation access to a black
consultant should be available and an opportunity sought to
open up the difficult issues which may be disabling both
workers and affecting their capacity to work together effectively.

The skills of group leadership

Leadership skills in groups are more diverse and manifold
than those involved when working with an individual. The
worker exercises her skills in four directions. These are
worker–member; member–member; worker–group; and
worker–external environment. With co-workers there is the
fifth direction discussed above: worker–worker.

These five directions can be shown diagrammatically for
an imaginary four-member group as in Fig. 3.2. The directions can be illustrated by considering one particular skill,
communication. The worker needs:

(a)   to establish effective communication, verbal and non-
      verbal, between herself and each individual group
      member;
(b)   to facilitate good communication between members;
(c)   to be able to communicate with the group as a whole,
      both at the task and feeling levels;
(d)   to be able to communicate with all the relevant
      external persons who can influence the group; and
(e)   to communicate well with her co-worker, if she has
      one.

Skills can be divided into *general skills* and *specific skills*.

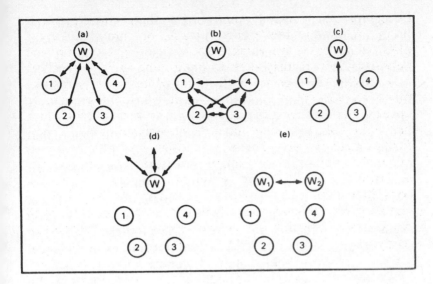

Fig. 3.2

General skills apply to all groups and can be categorised as the skills of group creation, group maintenance, group task achievement and group culture development. *Specific skills* are those needed for a particular type of group with its specific membership, aims and methods. Examples of specific skills are those associated with outdoor pursuits, activities and games, social skills training, psychodrama and sociodrama, discussion groups, community action groups, TA/Gestalt, assertiveness training, self-help, arts and crafts, residential group living, behaviour modification in groups, activation and illumination of the here-and-now. Specialist texts are recommended for detailed consideration of specific skills.

General skills will now be considered in more detail. Firstly, *group-creation skills* which were outlined in the last chapter. They apply only to specially formed groups, but there is an equivalent set of skills which applies to the first stages of work with any 'natural' group. This is the stage of making contact with the group and establishing a valid role and working relationship.

Secondly, there are *group-maintenance skills*. These are the skills associated with the group-maintenance functions listed previously. They involve developing and sustaining these functions over the life of the group. Maintenance skills are not easily articulated because much happens at the feeling level. The worker somehow communicates to the members her commitment to the group as a whole and to relating to each individual in it, and is sensitive to how they are feeling and experiencing group membership. She conveys 'therapeutic optimism', a realistic conviction that the group has the potential to achieve certain things for each member, and that membership can be satisfying and rewarding. The key attributes of empathy, genuineness and non-possessive warmth, identified in casework research by Truax and Carkhuff (1967), apply equally in groupwork. In a group the need is for each member to experience these qualities in the worker, who needs to create opportunities and 'space' for each person to feel sustained, valued and involved.

An overall maintenance skill is that of mobilising the therapeutic potential and attributes of each member in relation to the others and the shared task. One of the many structured ways of doing this is through co-counselling, when members work together in pairs for a while, each counselling/teaching/supporting the other. Another is when each individual is given space to contribute individually, whether through writing things down, talking in turn, or participating in an activity. How explicit these processes are made will depend on the type of group, but the need will always be there.

The level of trust in a group is a critical factor. Group-maintenance skills are aimed at developing group cohesion and the feeling of security which is a precondition for real trust. Groups often involve members in different kinds of risk-taking, when trust of self and others is put to the test.

The second aspect of group maintenance is sustaining group cohesion, once it is established, and particularly when relationships and individuals in the group are under threat. One way a group can be severely threatened is by erosion of its membership. This is most obvious in a closed group, with no opportunity for bringing in new members. Absent and fluctuating members often breed anxiety and uncertainty in a group, and the maintenance skill involves management of this, preferably by mobilising the collective responsibility of the group. The skill lies perhaps in communicating and demonstrating that group membership does matter, and carries responsibility. Absenteeism then becomes a cause for concern, rather than for either censure or disinterest. There are technical and ethical dilemmas about when to reach out, e.g. visiting an absent member at home, and when to 'allow' an individual to exercise responsibility for himself in his own way.

Absenteeism is only one of several problematic situations the worker may be faced with. Others involve the behaviour *in the group* of individual members who find themselves in particular roles, e.g. scapegoat, monopoliser, sub-grouper, disrupter, silent member, bore, casualty. The skills and the techniques needed in some of these situations, which depend in part on the worker's theoretical orientation (i.e. individual- or group-focused) will be described in the final section of the next chapter.

In summary, maintenance skills involve simultaneously responding to individual, interpersonal and group phenomena at the feeling level, thus facilitating the group process in ways which harness relationships and feelings for task-achievement purposes.

Thirdly there are *task-achievement skills*. These are skills associated with task-leadership functions. Many such skills are to do with programme development, the subject of the next chapter. Programme is what groups do, and how this is planned to achieve individual and group aims. It involves decisions about structure, planning and implementation. Some groups are much more obviously task-oriented than others, but instrumental skills are needed in all groups. For example, in a group designed to train members in welfare rights and advocacy skills, the task is relatively clear-cut – information is assembled, techniques are discussed and rehearsed. By contrast, a sensitivity or T-group has the task of studying behaviour in the here-and-now, as it happens. There is no planned agenda or activity, but the task is clear, and, *inter alia*, requires the worker to 'gate-keep' (the function of holding to task) if the members try to avoid it by discussing past history or extraneous matters.

A further cluster of task skills involves group assessment and analysis, evaluation, monitoring and recording. These skills are discussed in Chapter 7. There are also the external tasks of the groupworker. These include liaison with relevant persons and organisations, obtaining resources and ensuring optimal external conditions for the group.

Finally, there are *culture-development skills*. 'Once a group is a physical reality, the leader turns his (sic) energies to shaping the group into a therapeutic social system. He (sic) endeavours to establish a code of behavioural rules, or norms, which will guide the interaction of the group . . . it is the group which is the agent of change' (Yalom, 1975). This quote implies that the culture is largely determined by the worker. This may be true in group psychotherapy, which Yalom is discussing, but in social groupwork the expectation is that the group members largely determine the culture albeit influenced to varying degrees by the worker(s).

Group culture is a rather intangible concept, but a very real one. The skill lies in establishing norms and a positive culture which is empowering for the members. Role-modelling plays an important part in this as the members are more likely to be influenced by the worker's actions and what he communicates non-verbally than by what he says. For example, an interactional culture, involving the group as a mutual helping network, may be established by the worker demonstrating at a very early stage that mutual helping is to be valued. Instead of answering all questions that are directed at herself and producing all the ideas, she sets out to reduce this dependence on her as central person. She asks the opinions of different members and invites the group as a whole to answer questions directed at her, encouraging interchanges between members which do not directly involve herself.

A culture of openness, honesty and free expression of feelings can be fostered by the worker being open, honest, sharing *her* feelings, and reinforcing emergent expressions of this in the membership. If the desired culture involves responsible risk-taking (whether rock-climbing, sharing painful feelings or rehearsing a social skill), this behaviour will be modelled by the worker and reinforced in members. Another group cultural factor is respect for boundaries, whether of time, topic or persons. Culture-setting here involves good time-keeping, allowing each person to make his own contribution, and valuing confidentiality and trust.

Reid (1988) reminds us that it is commonplace to have fears about leading groups. He refers to anxieties about losing control, about resistant unresponsive members and a general fear of impotence. He mentions some of the common reactions to these anxieties such as being over-controlling, being inauthentic, misuse of techniques and gimmicks, a tendency to accentuate content and play down process, dependence on talking, and avoidance of confrontation. These are all fairly normal reactions. What can come with experience is a trust in the potential and ability of group members to help each other and to take a major share of the leadership. This will of course vary according to the context and membership, but it is generally true that most of us through fear of losing control do not allow sufficient space for the group members to exercise the degree of responsibility and skill which they are capable of.

Group leadership and self-disclosure

The subject of self-disclosure in groupwork and in other social work methods has not received much attention in the literature or on training courses. It is similarly neglected in related professions such as medicine, teaching and nursing. Exceptions are Yalom's helpful discussion of its use (1975, pp. 204–17) and some research into its content by Dies and Cohen (1976). The explanation of the general neglect lies perhaps more in its complexity and threatening nature than its lack of importance. There is evidence (Shulman, 1978; Truax and Carkhuff, 1967; Sainsbury, 1975; C. Brown, 1986) to support the view that the client's, user's or patient's perception of the professional helper as a person has a profound effect on the nature and extent of participation in 'treatment'.

What are the different kinds of self-disclosure? Firstly, its verbal and non-verbal dimensions can be distinguished. The social worker's general appearance, dress, manner, facial expressions and communicated feelings are a form of self-disclosure just as much as the spoken word. The group members *see* and *feel* the social worker as well as *hearing* him. Secondly, verbal self-disclosure may be the disclosure of personal *feelings*, 'I feel sad', or personal *information*, 'My wife died of cancer'. Thirdly, 'here-and-now' and 'there-and-then' disclosures are quite different in content and impact. The former are usually comments or feelings about the group and individuals in it: 'I feel very alienated from the group today' or 'John, I find it very annoying when you spoil the football game for everyone else.' There-and-then disclosures mostly refer to past experiences outside the group: 'I was out of work for six months once, so I know a bit what it's like.' Fourthly, there is self-disclosure about one's personal values, beliefs, or ideology: 'I'm against abortion because of my religion, but you must decide what is best for you.'

The aim of self-disclosure, as with any other technique, should be to help group members achieve their personal and group goals. It can be an effective way of role-modelling desired behaviour, e.g. if the groupworker expresses anxiety or anger, it is 'OK' for group members to express anxiety or anger; if the groupworker shares her personal experience as a parent it is 'OK' for members to do so too. A possible danger in role-modelling is when a comment which shows personal understanding is perceived as apparent endorsement of undesirable behaviour: 'I know what you feel, because when my baby screamed all night I hit him once or twice.' Another quality of self-disclosure is personal authenticity. The groupworker who presents as a 'real' person with outside relationships and normal human strengths and frailties, has credibility and is less likely to reinforce members' fantasies about her. This kind of sharing of self is very different from the leader on an ego trip, whose 'performance' and personal revelations may be admired and enjoyed by the members, but do nothing for their problems and needs.

In contemplating the use of self-disclosure in a group, the practitioner needs to consider the *context*, the *type* of self-disclosure and the *timing*. The *context* refers to the type of group, the model it is based on, and its aims. At one extreme is the encounter group whose ethos is maximum personal disclosure and total authenticity. The worker in such a group who discloses nothing of himself will rapidly lose credibility. Conversely, in a positive peer-culture group where the main thrust is within the peer-group, and the worker's role is deliberately circumscribed, extensive self-disclosure would be quite inappropriate.

Regarding the *types* of self-disclosure outlined above, the

Dies and Cohen research indicated that there-and-then disclosures are generally experienced as less threatening than here-and-now revelations, particularly when the latter involve negative feedback to individuals as distinct from general expressions of feeling about the self or the group.

Timing is very important. Extensive use of self-disclosure in the early stages of a group is not helpful, particularly expressions of self-doubt about the group. At that stage the members are usually looking to the worker as a reliable strong person who shows conviction about what he or she is doing, and who can cope. They are not, however, seeking a superwoman or superman, and some relatively non-threatening disclosure of personal vulnerability at an early stage can be reassuring. An example of this was a first meeting of a men's group. There was a tense silence and an awkwardness when the first session was due to begin. The worker said he expected everyone was feeling rather anxious as he certainly was. This had the immediate effect of relaxing the tension in the group, shown by the taking off of jackets, and more relaxed postures. The worker had modelled 'it's OK to be anxious'.

Once the group is well established as a cohesive unit with leadership being shared by the members, more potentially threatening forms of worker self-disclosure may be risked, provided these are primarily for the benefit of the members and not the worker. For example, an Intermediate Treatment group, which has been running for several months, goes away for a week's camp. At the camp the context is different: it becomes a group-living situation (as in residential work, see Chapter 5), the group is well established and it may be very important for the children to experience their social workers as 'real' people with normal human foibles. Many social workers speak of the deeper relationships and trust which develop from this kind of exposure and mutual encounter as 'real' people.

Finally, self-disclosure is not just a matter of learned techniques. It depends on the social worker's feelings about herself as she actually is, and her confidence in using all the parts of herself in her work. For some people this state comes naturally, but for most it requires training and structured experiences in group membership.

4 Group Programme and Group Process

This chapter is concerned with what happens in groups, and how this can be influenced by programme. All groups have natural processes or group dynamics, and the skill of the groupworker lies in developing a programme of activities which phase in with the stages and condition of the group, to provide the best possible opportunities for task achievement. The term 'activities' is used here in the broadest sense, to describe anything which a group may be engaged in from talking together, to playing games, to meeting with a local authority official. Each group model influences the choice of activities, as does any working agreement about aims and methods. Our general assumption however is that groupworkers need to be flexible and pragmatic in their use of programme, drawing on different sources and ideas.

The following sections will discuss the concept of programme, and the general considerations and questions which arise; the natural process of groups and the stages of development which they may follow; the range of activities available for programme planning, and some of their possible uses; and finally, some indications of programme technique which can be used to help manage problematic situations, including scapegoating and 'stuck groups'.

Programme – the concept and some general considerations

Programme as a concept and working tool is not prominent in the groupwork literature (but see Briscoe, 1978; Heap, 1979; Middleman, 1980; Ross and Thorpe, 1988; Phillips, 1989). This may be because it tends to be equated with a structured goal-oriented approach. In reality, every group has a programme if we define it as *what the group does as a means of trying to achieve its aims.* With this definition, a decision to run a group on an existential creative spontaneity basis is as much a programme decision as is an elaborate timetable of visits, talks and structured activities. There is a distinction to be made between *potential* or *planned* programme and *actual* programme. The former is what is planned in advance, the latter is what the group actually does, and the two do not always coincide!

Some basic considerations affect decisions about programme. The first two are philosophical as well as technical:

(a) *Structure and spontaneity.* Every group has to reach some balance between prearranged structure and spontaneous development. Some groups are so preplanned and rigid that there is no scope for response to the needs of individual members and their unique group. Others are so vague and unstructured that they drift along aimlessly, without anyone really knowing what they are there for, or what they are supposed to be doing. Groups need both the security of some known structure, and the flexibility necessary for learning and change.

(b) *Person and task.* Every group is concerned with its members as people, and with the tasks for which it is met. A group with person-centred aims, as in group psychotherapy, is likely to devise a person-centred programme. A group which is highly task-oriented, whether that task is located at the individual, group or community level, is likely to devise a programme emphasising procedures, decisions and the monitoring of task achievement. Most social work groups require a sensitive balance between focus on persons and focus on task. This is one reason why programming is a highly skilled aspect of groupwork.

(c) *Individual factors.* Programme depends on what the members are capable of, and this varies according to age, verbal ability, practical ability, motivation and self-control. In groups with a wide ability range, programme needs to include activities adaptable to individual differences.

(d) *Group factors.* Programme takes into account fixed

factors such as group composition and size, and variable factors associated with the stage of development the group has reached, and its current state. This includes group morale, cohesion, conflict and the level of commitment to task.

(e) *The individual and the group*. Programme should be consistent with what has been agreed with individuals and the group in the initial contract, although as a group develops, needs and interests change, and opportunities for renegotiating programme should be available. Programme involves a blending of activities which include the whole group with those which individuals undertake on their own, or in pairs, or subgroups. As a guideline, individual and pairs activities may be more needed in the early stages when group experience is rather daunting for some members.

(f) *Resources*. Many activities need resources, both cash and in kind. This may be a real limitation on programme, and it is unethical to raise members' expectations about exciting activities unless necessary resources will be available.

Given these basic considerations, the groupworker then faces a number of questions.

What will the group actually do?

Traditionally, groupwork has relied heavily on the use of discussion and a limited range of other activities. A much wider range of possibilities is now available (as will be seen later in this chapter) and this is constantly being added to by the creativity of groupworkers and members. The choice within this range is dependent not only on the task, resources and member capabilities, but also on the skills and capability of the groupworker. Group members are quick to sense whether the worker feels comfortable with the methods she is using, and if she reveals excessive anxiety and uncertainty it will be transmitted rapidly to others. It may make them reluctant to engage in the activity, and more vulnerable to failure. Groupworkers wishing to extend their repertoire of activities and skills by trying out a new approach for the first time, can usually do so with more confidence if they have rehearsed it beforehand in the relatively 'safe' setting of the team or a training session, perhaps using video play-back.

Who makes programme decisions and how are they made?

The agency, the worker(s) and the group members all play a part in programme decisions. Agency influence is exerted through general policy and control of resources. Within these constraints, decisions depend on negotiations between workers and members. A combination of worker anxiety and member dependency sometimes results in a worker-selected programme in the early stages. This may be helpful initially, but there is the danger of establishing a dependency pattern in which members' own ideas and wishes are not valued. If a worker opts for an approach which offers members a significant say in what the programme will be, a group decision-making process becomes necessary. The management of this requires considerable skill as the worker balances group aims and her own ideas and wishes with those of group members which may diverge. Both worker and members need to be clear about which decisions are negotiable and how any conflicts will be resolved.

A simple example of this is seen in the programme decision about when group meetings will be held. At one group this was to be decided at the initial contract-making meeting. The two co-workers knew which evenings they would prefer, Friday not being one of them. When it came to deciding, one of the group members took it upon himself to organise a vote to see which evening was the most popular. Friday won the vote, and the workers found themselves having to rearrange personal programmes to accommodate the group decision. Their first 'mistake' was not making it clear that certain evenings were not negotiable, the second was not questioning voting as a means of making decisions, there having been no group agreement to use voting in this way. They were confused about the nature of their authority in that group, and how much power they could or indeed wanted to wield. On the positive side, the members got an early message that contract-making was a genuine process in which their interests counted.

In group decision-making processes the more reticent members can be dominated by the more assertive and articulate. The worker may need to devise methods which allow each individual to express her views freely, and to ensure that those views are given equal consideration.

How much is planned in advance?

Some activities require much more forward-planning than others. A week's camp, a meeting with the local police inspector or an invitation to another group for a meal, all need varying degrees of advance preparation. So does the use of video, as the equipment has to be obtained, set-up and checked. A trust exercise, role-play or walk needs less preplanning, although the worker himself still needs to be adequately prepared.

These are the practicalities of planning ahead, but which activities and approaches are best suited for different stages of the group's life? To assess this, an understanding of how groups develop and change over a period of time is needed.

Group processes and stages of development

Group process has been defined by Garvin (1974) as 'those changes occurring in the activities and interactions of group members that are related to changes in goal attainment and group maintenance'. One of the most profound characteristics of group process is the way in which the whole mood and functioning of a group, the roles, behaviour, communication patterns and interaction of the members can and do change quite dramatically over a period of time. These changes have been studied by researchers (Sarri and Galinsky, 1974; Garland, Jones and Kolodny, 1965; Schutz, 1958; Tuckman, 1965) who have identified the typical stages of most groups. Hartford (1971) includes the *pre-group* stage, sub-divided into 'private' (someone has the idea) and 'public' (active promotion of a group) phases. There are *linear* models of group development in which one stage follows the next progressively, *cyclical* models (Schutz, 1958), and *helical* versions which combine linear and cyclical tendencies in a spiralling concept. Whilst the linear approach is an over-simplification (every group has setbacks and periods of regression) it is a useful starting point and we shall therefore follow Tuckman's stages of *forming, storming, norming and performing* with the addition of the final stage of *ending*, or if you prefer the rhyme, *mourning!* Each of these stages will now be discussed in turn, indicating their significance for both group maintenance and group task/activity, and what this suggests for worker behaviour and programme.

Forming

This is the stage when the group first starts. Initially, it is a collection of individuals, each of whom will be preoccupied with issues to do with *joining* or *inclusion*. They will be drawing on their past experience of other groups, searching for similarities and looking round for other individuals with whom they may feel some affinity (isn't that what you do when you join a new group?) At the emotional level, behaviour is often characterised by approach-avoidance movements, as new members 'dip their toes in the water' tentatively exploring the group's attractiveness and the limits on what they personally can do. There is often much dependence on the worker and an apparent willingness to conform to whatever is suggested. Sometimes an extrovert individual is very active and talkative, making a successful but often temporary bid for the leadership. Another member may start by pouring out personal problems or views before s/he or the group is ready to deal with them. At the task level, there may be reluctance by members to take responsibility for helping to plan the programme and decide on individual and group goals. Discussion may ramble and become anecdotal. These behaviours are quite common in the initial stages of many groups, but are likely to be more pronounced when members have not been in a formed group before. The groupworker can easily underestimate the anxiety this new experience can produce for the individual who has not yet learned *how to function in the role of group member*. It takes time and experience to discover how you as a member can use a group to benefit yourself and other members.

The forming stage will be affected by whether the group is a 'stranger' group (in which all start from the same baseline) or a group in which some or all the members already know each other, whether through previous agency contact – perhaps another group – living in the same neighbourhood, being part of the same family or social network or for any other reason. This introduces a 'past history' into the group which will inevitably affect present role-expectations and group behaviour, not least if some members have had an individual work relationship with the worker and others have not. Some of these previous relationships will not only be obvious, but will be openly declared, perhaps in the form of sub-groupings, cliques or a member claiming a special relationship with the worker. Others will be hidden perhaps because of embarrassment (as in one group when one member found herself sitting next to another who was the childminder for her children and knew details of her personal life – she later withdrew), antipathy or uncertainty. Secret relationships within a group are at best constraining and at worst destructive, and it is therefore desirable as a general guideline to encourage the open acknowledgement of these relationships at an early stage in the group's life. There will, however, be occasions when for reasons of confidentiality, privacy or at a member's request it is not appropriate to encourage disclosure. The skill of the worker is in using the sociometry of the group as a positive force for group development and task achievement. The initial programme can be arranged, for example, with the deliberate choice of activities in which members work in stranger pairs or sub-groupings for a while. Sub-groupings can promote a positive basis for group cohesion if that energy contributes to the group as a whole and is not encapsulated or split off. The worker also needs to demonstrate verbally that she is equally concerned with all members, whether or not she knew some of them before.

Another possibility is that everyone in a 'new' group already knows each other, as may happen in a residential setting, or an institutional setting such as a prison, a school or a social work training course. In these settings the task of the worker at the forming stage is concerned with a more complicated joining process. She needs to establish a clear purpose and boundary for the group, separating it but not isolating it from the normal life of the institution. This can be facilitated by careful choice of location, and by a task and programme which is manifestly different from other things done outside the group. The members will need help in freeing themselves from expected roles and behaviour patterns, and in using their group experience and learning in the rest of their group-living experience. If the worker is a member of staff in the establishment there will be dual-role problems, particularly if she is in some formal authority role. This should be openly acknowledged. In a residential setting, the programme of any specific group should be seen as part of an integrated twenty-four-hour programme for the whole establishment, with staff working as a team, supporting one another in the different roles they carry. If the staff can collaborate across these boundaries whilst still maintaining them, then the residents have a chance of 'mirroring' their behaviour and doing likewise.

The groupworker's task at the first meeting of a new group has several basic components, the emphasis and chronological order varying according to the type of group:

(*1*) To facilitate introductions and help the members to join together to form a group which is attractive to them and to which they feel some commitment. This may be done by the use of some suitable structures and exercises (see next section) which involve members from the beginning in active participation with each other, and as a group.

(*2*) To make a clear statement about why the group has been formed, and how its purpose is viewed by the workers and the agency, allowing space and time for the members to respond and express their views.

(*3*) To 'clear expectations' with members about why they have come, what they would like to do and what they are hoping to gain from the group.

(*4*) To negotiate and agree the group contract (see Chapter 2), including the way in which members will work together and any group 'rules'. If attendance is non-voluntary, the implications of this need to be clear.

(*5*) To discuss the group programme and methods to be used and to consider what is planned to happen at the next meeting.

(*6*) To indicate the way the worker(s) hopes to work with the group and what her role will be.

(7) To begin to establish group culture, for example the philosophy of a mutual aid system and shared responsibility.

In some groups some of these aspects will only be touched upon at a first meeting. For a lucid account of worker skills in the beginning stage of a group see Shulman (1984, chaps 9 and 10).

Another variation on 'forming' is the re-forming which is necessary when a new member joins an already existing group. Anyone who has experienced this when taking a new post in an existing work team will know how difficult the joining can be, and how important the initial reactions of the group are. There is the 'ghost' of any person who has been replaced to contend with, plus the culture and past history of the group before you joined it. The new member's feelings are likely to include both a wish for recognition and a fear of early exposure in a new culture. This anxiety may show in a low profile or an assertion of self ('you've got to notice me'). The programme should include advance preparation of the group and the newcomer for the change. In some groups the members contribute to the decision about a new person joining and they are likely to be more receptive if they feel the newcomer has not been imposed on them. An introduction and procedures which establish the newcomer as a group member in the reformed group whilst allowing him to ease his way in gradually, can be helpful. Galinsky and Schopler (1985) have researched the patterns of entry and exit in open groups and identified useful guidelines for practitioners.

Storming (and depression?)

This is a critical stage in the group's development, and it can be make-or-break. It is the point at which members are beginning to seek individual roles and space, and conflict can arise as they jockey for position and search for compatible roles within the group. Issues of control and power are prominent, and these may be tested in worker–member as well as member–member interactions. Anyone who feels she has been coerced into the group is likely to reveal this in some way. For some members, or even for the group as a whole, the 'fight' may turn inward and show as depression or 'flight'. Members often arrive at a new group with unrealistically high expectations, and a depressed feeling after a few sessions can result from the realisation that the group offers no magical solutions to problems, but that any gain is likely to involve personal investment and effort.

After initial fears of not belonging, the opposite fear of group absorption and loss of individual significance may surface. Personal needs and aspirations have to be compromised if a culture of sharing is to develop in which each member's needs are to be expressed and met. The worker is likely to experience conflicting messages of both dependence ('Please lead us through this confusion and control us') and independence ('This is our group now, and we intend to challenge your leadership and power').

At the task level, there may be anxiety and uncertainty about what individuals can achieve and how the group can help them. It is therefore very important that all members get involved in group activity, and experience some initial success and progress at this stage. This suggests activities which are relatively non-threatening, undemanding and well within the capabilities of members. If the group is stuck in verbal deadlock, a change of emphasis may be needed to involve members in other ways, perhaps through games and simulations or some of the easier drama therapy techniques. 'Positive feedback' from self, other members and worker(s) provides the necessary reinforcement and encouragement to continue. This applies equally to a psychotherapeutic group, a social skills group or a community action group, e.g. when a recently formed tenants' group is facing political pressure from a powerful housing department, it is crucial that initial tasks are manageable and have a good expectation of success. Ambitious unrealistic goals, such as trying to change a policy overnight, can only result in disillusionment and quite possibly the demise of the group.

The group is still quite fragile, and the worker may need to demonstrate security by controlling individual members if they test the limits. This requires a firm but sensitive approach aimed at reducing unhelpful conflict. P. Smith (1978) suggests that the worker needs to seek an appropriate balance between confrontation and support, avoiding any polarisation of these two approaches.

The 'storming' stage can be rather difficult for the novice groupworker, particularly if the members are also inexperienced in groups. In these circumstances an experienced co-worker and/or supervision and support are necessary. The more experienced worker is also likely to be anxious, but can develop a time perspective which reminds him or her that this often happens in groups, and that remaining relatively calm and optimistic should help the members. Similarly, an experienced group member can be a great help to the worker, communicating a realistic confidence that the group will develop and that members will begin to achieve some of the things they hoped for when they joined.

Note: Suggestions about ways of responding to the kinds of difficulties that may arise at this stage are discussed later on in this chapter.

Norming

When the group has successfully sorted out some of the issues of power and control, it is freed to develop trust, cohesion and a degree of intimacy. The group begins to be important to the members, relationships matter, and emotional investment in 'our group' develops. Group culture emerges. Part of this process is the establishment of norms, or accepted ways of doing things, and agreement about sanctions and where the limits are.

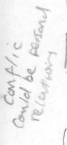

At the emotional level, individuals may start sharing more of themselves, and if conflicts arise they may be in the area of personal relationships and attractions. The stability which is established may be at the cost of one or more members carrying 'scapegoat' roles, and if this causes the worker to feel the need to challenge the apparent harmony, she is likely to be unpopular. This is because a feature at this stage is a tendency for the group to become an end in itself for the members. The worker's aim is to try to harness this group togetherness and cohesion for task achievement. One way of doing this is by steadily increasing the members' participation and investment in programme decisions and implementation.

The point at which group members begin to take respons-

ibility, individually and collectively, for the group and its tasks, is the point when they are ready to 'perform'. This stage is often a watershed or breakthrough in a group's progress. For the worker, it is like having a weight lifted from her shoulders. Programme design can now encourage the taking of risks in the direction of change. In a gestalt group this might mean taking the 'hot seat' and working at difficult painful areas of personal development. In a positive peer-culture group it could mean confronting a peer-leader if he is deviating from acceptable behaviour. In a social skills group it could mean agreeing to test interviewee skills in a real interview. In a community group it could mean chairing an important meeting for the first time, or having a dialogue with a councillor on the radio. In a residential group it could mean behaving in ways which risk a comeback from others outside the group. In a single-parent group it could mean sharing feelings about loneliness.

Some models refer to a 'revision stage' or cyclical effect when a group has a set-back, or crisis of some kind. This could be at the emotional level, as when one member's behaviour causes others to seek to remove her from the group, or at the task level if an individual or group project fails. These occasions can be used by workers and the group as opportunities for reviewing progress and reassessing the programme. A stocktaking session can be very productive and serve as a springboard for the next move forward.

Programme design during the life of a group needs increasingly to stress the links between what members do in the group and their functioning in the 'real world' (in some group models, for example the self-directed social action model outlined by Mullender and Ward (1991), the primary task is about change in the external environment of the group). One effective way of doing this is the use of *assignments* or homework, in which members identify tasks to work at or try out between sessions, perhaps with support from other group members, with agreement to report back to the next meeting. This emphasises that the group is a means to an end, and not (in most cases) an end in itself. A danger to be avoided if possible is allocating tasks which put too much pressure on individuals, bringing fear of failure, and sometimes making it difficult for them to return to the group.

Performing

Much performing occurs at the norming stage, and the distinction is one of emphasis only. Performing is the point at which the group becomes a largely self-sufficient resource, using all the skills and potential of the members to achieve its aims and solve problems. It is likely to have an enabling structure and a high level of cohesion and trust. In some groups, e.g. self-help, mutual support, or community-based, this may be the point at which the group becomes autonomous and takes on its own identity, independent of the social workers and the agency. It may serve as a model for other groups to learn from and emulate. Many groups (particularly short-life groups) do not reach this stage.

Ending

Most groups come to an end. Many have a fixed time span, known from the beginning, others end when the task is completed or when there seems no purpose in continuation. Some are continuous but with changing membership, so they have individual endings, but not a group ending.

We shall first consider group endings. These are characterised by various predictable feelings and behaviour. Frequently group members want to postpone the ending by continuing beyond the agreed date. There is a belief that if only there were more time, all the goals could be achieved. A modified version of this is a wish to have periodic 'reunions'. These pressures are quite seductive because they may have some validity, but workers and members need to be cautious when considering negotiating an extension (often only some members really want it, and then attendance may be poor and motivation lacking). There may be euphoria that much has been achieved, or the opposite extreme, a discounting of achievements. There is sometimes depression about the loss of 'what might have been' and sadness at the ending of the group and the personal relationships.

The worker has several programme responsibilities connected with group ending. The first is to make it clear from the beginning that the group has a limited life (if it has), and periodically to remind members of this as the group develops. Secondly, she needs to help members to link group activities and experience to their outside 'real' world and to do this increasingly as the group approaches its end. Thirdly, she needs to help members to evaluate realistically what they and the group have achieved and have failed to achieve. This process should be started some time before the final session so members have a period of mental preparation and adjustment. There may be tangible evidence to draw on, such as something they have made, improved school attendance, travelling on a bus (for an agoraphobic), obtaining a community resource or obtaining a job. Fourthly, there may be 'unfinished business', perhaps between members, or members and workers. It is important to create opportunities, for example through the use of feedback exercises, for this to be acknowledged and if possible resolved before the group disperses or an individual leaves. Fifthly, individual members may need assistance in planning continuation and consolidation of development and achievement after the group ends. This involves working out ways of replacing the group by other community support systems. These could include other group members, family, volunteers, clubs, other groups or some form of continuing social work help. The whole emphasis is on the group not being an isolated experience for the individual, but a process which is linked to their social functioning.

Groups often suggest some kind of ritual ending such as a party, a trip or an evening in the pub. As with other rituals which are concerned with role transition, this can be very useful as a visible ending and marking of the boundary between group and no group.

Group endings are often quite difficult for the group-worker because he too feels the emotion and sadness (sometimes accompanied by relief which he may feel guilty about!) A good way to deal with this is by openly acknowledging it in the group. The worker role-models 'it's OK to be sad'. The powerful influence of group atmosphere is never more evident than at the time of ending. Programme can help by ensuring that every individual has the space and time to disengage from each of the other members and the worker.

When a group ends prematurely because of 'failure' (e.g. lack of members, task not achieved, no more funds), the worker(s) have a special responsibility to try to help members cope with the mixture of feelings of anger, sadness, relief and frustration. At the same time, they may be struggling with their own disappointment, they in turn needing support from colleagues and supervisor.

Individual endings in a continuing group are obviously much easier when the reason is goal achievement than when it is some kind of failure or incompatibility. The programme skill lies in making space for the individual to evaluate her progress (including feedback from other members), and disengage emotionally from the group, whilst the group's work for the remaining members continues. One device for doing this is to establish a leaving ritual in which every member has a right to participate. In some groups, especially those with a peer-culture emphasis, the decision about individual withdrawal is viewed as a matter for the group as a whole, just as individual joining of a continuous group may be a group decision. This model has the advantage of a built-in disengagement process. As with other group phenomena, one individual's leaving predicament resonates for others, motivating them to think about their membership and progress. This can be both unsettling and productive.

Readers wishing to pursue the topic of group endings in more depth are directed to an article by Ross (1991) in which she describes and analyses some of the behavioural and psychological responses to ending, illustrated with examples from groups for children and adolescents.

We have concentrated here on Tuckman's linear model, but brief mention should also be made of Schutz's cyclical model (Schutz, 1958). He identifies three key aspects of group development: *inclusion, control* and *affection*. In his model the initial stage of a new group is characterised by a preoccupation with belonging and *inclusion*. As in Tuckman's forming stage, group members are tentatively – or not so tentatively – seeking links and interaction with others. They are often ambivalent about inclusion because it may mean both pleasure and pain, both new opportunities and new responsibilities. The second stage is about *control* and the issues identified as storming by Tuckman. The authority, competence and skill of the worker may be tested and power struggles develop among peers. When this difficult stage is worked through, closer relationships develop between members, the stage of *affection*. The cyclical phenomenon now develops because intimacy for some, as in a close pairing between two members, can mean a feeling of exclusion for others. This raises the inclusion issue again, albeit in a different guise. And so the cycle is repeated but in a more sophisticated form this time. Schutz suggested that for effective ending the cycle needs to be reversed, with members first disengaging from the bonds of affection, then freeing themselves from controlling and being controlled, and lastly reversing inclusion by the ultimate exclusion that occurs for all – in a fixed-life group – when the group no longer exists to belong to.

Two general points need to be made about the Tuckman, Schutz and other models of group stages. The first is that to a degree the same series of stages are experienced within every group meeting, as well as over the full life of the group. Each time a group reconvenes there will to some extent be a reforming, an adjustment, an acknowledgement of the 'rules of the game', a period of 'work', an evaluation and an ending. The second point is a word of caution. All groups are different, and the phases of development will depend, *inter alia*, on 'the particular needs of members, the type of setting in which they meet and the orientation of the leader in that group' (P.Smith, 1978). There is *no* suggestion that every group follows the above stages in a neat progression, whether linear or cyclical.

Most of these models are extrapolated from studies of groups in general, and merely offer guidelines. Stages always overlap, and the intermediate ones follow no clear sequence. What can safely be said is that most groups have beginnings, middles and ends; that characteristic behaviours are associated with each of these stages; and that programme planning and activities must take account of these characteristics. There will always be variations as between stranger and non-stranger groups, open and closed groups, and field and residential settings. The reader who wishes to study another model is encouraged to read Garland, Jones and Kolodny (1965), who in addition to describing and illustrating the stages of development in children's groups, also discuss conceptual and practice issues.

Group activities and techniques

Vinter (Glasser, Sarri and Vinter, 1974, Chapter 13) suggests that group activities can be analysed into six general factors.

(1) *Prescriptiveness.* Activities vary in the extent to which they prescribe an individual's behaviour (e.g. open discussion is low in prescriptiveness, but a game of badminton is high).

(2) *Controls.* The sources of control vary between the individual, other group members, the worker and the rules (e.g. football has its rules and the control of the referee; psychodrama has the control of the drama-therapist; an unstructured swimming session relies heavily on individual self-control; a guided group interaction session places control mainly with the peer group, but with the worker as back-up).

(3) *Physical movement* is central to some activities (e.g. bioenergetic exercises), and peripheral to others (e.g. a discussion group).

(4) *Competence and skill.* The demands on a group member's ability can be varied by choice of activity (e.g. rock climbing, clay modelling, trust exercises), and within the range of a particular activity (e.g. climbing a simple practice rock, negotiating a severe overhang).

(5) *Participant interaction.* Activities vary from those which are individualised (e.g. writing your own ideas down on a piece of paper), to those which require maximum group interaction (e.g. a sociodrama re-enactment of a court scene).

(6) *Reward structure.* Activities have their pains and pleasures. They can be rewarding tangibly ('I made that cake'), or less tangibly ('I feel really good after our group meeting').

Davies (1975) mentions a seventh factor, to do with the degree of creativity: e.g. a role-play with scripted roles is more limiting on creativity than a guided group fantasy in which anything (or almost anything!) goes. Phillips (1989) draws on Vinter's framework to analyse the 'targeted' use of group activities in a day centre for people recovering from mental illness.

With Vinter's general factors in mind, we shall now describe the range of group activities and techniques, and then consider briefly the matching of programme content to group aims, constraints, value-base and objectives of the agency, and group processes (Ross and Thorpe, 1988).

Name-learning techniques

In any stranger group, name-learning is a top priority in the joining process, and it is often accompanied by some brief information about the person, if they wish to divulge it. In a group larger than six, the conventional approach of asking each person in turn can be quite threatening, and also a fairly ineffective way of learning. Variations include: starting off in pairs, exchanging names and brief information, and then introducing each other to the group; going round the circle naming yourself and your neighbours; or finding your name pinned on someone else's back. One very effective method is playing catch with a soft object and calling the name of the person you throw it to, culminating in each person going right round the circle. This can be done sitting down, or moving around. One good way of getting to know a bit about the person as well as their name is to ask them to reflect on their name, how they acquired it, what they feel about it, and what they prefer to be called. This can be surprisingly revealing bringing in information about ethnic roots, family patterns, likes and dislikes, and therefore needs to be used sensitively. The worker's participation and role-modelling in these early exercises is important, as is her awareness of the approach likely to work best with a particular group.

Trust exercises

These are used particularly in the early stages of some person-centred groups, but may be used at any time. Some are done in pairs, e.g. falling backwards and a partner catching you, and the 'blind walk' in which one person leads another blindfold, without talking, for five or ten minutes, and then the roles are reversed. Other trust exercises involve the whole group together, as when the group forms a close circle and an individual stands in the centre, eyes closed, and is supported as he or she sways to and fro in a gradually widening circle. It is important to allow time after each exercise or sequence of exercises for expression of feeling and for discussion. Groupworkers need to be comfortable themselves about doing these kinds of exercises and sensitive to members' feelings about doing them, and there needs to be an explicit understanding that participation is voluntary. Some people find any form of physical touch extremely threatening, and are likely to prefer to explore trust in other ways. Many examples of trust exercises are described in Brandes and Phillips (1978), and Ernst and Goodison (1982).

Talking

There are many variations on talking in a group. The *co-counselling* or tandem method, when members work for a while in pairs, can be very productive, and in larger groups offers a welcome time of personal attention, a form of refuge from group pressures. This pairing can either be very prescriptive ('One of you speak to the other for two minutes about things you do well, and then reverse roles for two minutes'), or more open ('Share with each other how you feel about yourself and the group today'). The issue of selection of a partner for any paired activity in a group is a sensitive one and can be either random, freely chosen or chosen according to some criterion. Random methods may be less threatening in the early stages. When numbers are odd, the worker must judge whether one threesome or a pairing with herself would be most appropriate. Co-workers can model co-counselling with each other, or observe the members.

At group level the variations revolve around structure and aims. Discussion can be either completely unstructured (you speak when you feel like it), or structured so that each individual has a turn, or some blend of the two. Periodic structure to give each individual space can be productive, and also an effective way of involving 'silent' members who often find some structure makes active participation a bit easier. Discussion in sub-groups is another variation.

The worker needs to learn the natural language and communication styles of the members as important background to the programme. Conversely, certain activities and therapeutic models have a language which members need to learn and use, e.g. in a rock climbing group technical terms such as belay and abseil; in a transactional analysis group key words and phrases such as critical parent, scripts, stroking, adapted child, stamp-collection and 'not OK'. In positive peer-culture groups, members learn a vernacular of problems such as 'low self-image', 'inconsiderate of others', 'authority problem' and 'fronting'. These models are distinguished from traditional psychotherapy and behaviour modification which also have their language (e.g. counter-transference, desensitisation), but this language is usually reserved for the therapists.

Writing

This is a very important activity in a group. It can be used by members at the individual level for self-positioning, self-assessment and goal-setting; periodic evaluation, reflection and ideas; and personal recording. Blank sheets can be used accompanied by verbal guidelines, or written instructions used for sentence completion, questionnaires, scales, checklists, or the snakes and ladders of personal history and aspirations. Many of these exercises are described by Priestley *et al.* in *Social Skills and Personal Problem Solving* (1978). Writing can also be a group activity, using a blackboard or large sheets of plain paper and felt-pens. The purpose may be brainstorming (aimed at producing a large number of ideas on a chosen topic), constructing a group contract and programme, planning a meeting or trip, making a recipe, etc.

Periodic individual or group writing sessions have value as a variation on discussion, and can be used to obtain a change in tempo or emphasis. Writing creates time and space for people to express their thoughts and feelings in a different way. A disadvantage is that some people may find writing very difficult, and should not be exposed or embarrassed. Groupworkers need to be very sensitive to this, but should not underestimate what each individual can achieve with help from them and other members.

Refreshments, cooking, eating and drinking

If refreshments or a meal are to be part of the programme, the timing, arrangements and content are important. Some groups have refreshments either before or after the group session, and they may thereby signify the social/work time boundary. Others, particularly children's groups and half-day or longer groups, use refreshments during the proceedings, perhaps to separate different activities, or to build in a period of relaxation and informal interchange. Providing refreshments is also a direct and valuable form of caring. As the group develops, members themselves often like to share responsibility for the preparation.

Learning how to cook may be a programme activity with both therapeutic and skill-development elements. A woman probation officer ran a very successful 'pie-making' group for male offenders in their late teens. Although quite tough and sophisticated in crime, they committed themselves enthusiastically to weekly pie-making sessions, becoming proficient at the skills, but also sharing of themselves and their problems with each other and the probation officer in the process. Walker (1978) in her lucid account of a Family Service Unit (FSU) parents' group describes how an invitation to eat a meal prepared by a rival FSU group stimulated her group to include planning and preparation of lunch as a central feature of their programme. Walker points out how cooking meals together developed individual skills, social interaction and a capacity to plan ahead.

Social skills techniques

Groups provide a supportive forum for developing social skills. There is the opportunity for role-play and rehearsal of skills including interview technique, assertiveness training, handling frustration, saying 'no', managing personal relationships, interacting at a party, coping with the boss, managing anger without becoming violent and many others. Everyone has skills to develop, and there are roles for all group members in the role-plays and offering feedback. The various techniques are described in detail in Priestley *et al.* (1978) and Bond (1986).

Psychodrama

Psychodrama (Gale, 1990) is one of several drama-based techniques which use live enactment of personal or social experiences. It has much to offer groupworkers, and Blatner's *Acting-in* (1973) gives a clear exposition of 'practical applications of psychodramatic methods'. In psychodrama the individual is helped to enact her problem instead of just talking about it. The emphasis on non-verbal communication, movement and experience, makes it a particularly effective medium for children, people with learning difficulties, inarticulate people, over-intellectualisers and some categories of offenders and psychiatric patients. The structured group experience provides the context for enactment designed to turn acting-out impulses into insights and a capacity to make better use of feelings. Group members take roles such as 'doubling' (representing the alter-ego of the problem-presenter, speaking the unspoken thoughts and feelings) and 'auxiliary egos' (significant others) in the individual's psychodrama. Most groupworkers will not become psychodrama therapists, but the techniques offer much scope for creative adaptation in different forms of groupwork.

Sociodrama

Sociodrama (Jennings, 1973) works on similar principles to psychodrama, but the focus is on a context of social interaction rather than on an individual's personal 'problem'. Thus an adolescent group may be asked to become an imaginary family facing some typical crisis, e.g. a fourteen-year-old girl staying out very late at night, and to dramatise it. Or they may re-enact an actual juvenile court or school classroom scene that some of them have experienced, each taking roles in the sociodrama. It is less personally threatening than psychodrama and offers an experiential approach to social learning. In all these drama techniques, the role of the facilitator at the warm-up stage is crucial in creating an atmosphere of trust and spontaneity. Dramatherapy in a mixed programme can also energise members for other group activities (Jennings 1987).

Sculpting

This is another creative technique, also used in family therapy. People in a group are placed in a physical representation or 'sculpt' of their emotional relatedness, as seen by one member of that group. It can be used either to recreate an external group (family or other) to which one or more members belong, or to sculpt the group itself in the here-and-now. In a group sculpt, individuals may be able to show how they feel about themselves and the group in ways which they could not verbalise. When people are in position in a sculpt they can be asked how they feel and how they would like it to be different. This can illustrate vividly how a move by one person has consequences for others, e.g. if A moves out of the scapegoat position, who will take her or his place? In sculpting, as with most experiential activities, it is essential to allow time for members to 'de-role' and discuss their experience. Strong feelings may be engendered which need to be worked through before the session ends.

Audio-visual aids

Video has various uses in groups, including skill development, fun and community action. It is a particularly powerful medium for accurate direct feedback in social skills training, and portable video cameras can be used by community and other groups to do interviews and make films relevant to their group and community goals. Video can be great fun, and also quite threatening, not to mention frustrating when it does not work properly! For all these reasons, its use in group programme requires care and planning. (Its use in groupwork training is discussed in Chapter 7.)

Another creative visual technique which is being developed by DeVere and Rhonne (1991) involves the use of Photo-Language (PL). Group members are shown carefully chosen still photographs and asked to respond to them. Subjective interpretation of these photographic images can be used to elicit and examine both individual and group attitudes and emotions. DeVere and Rhonne give an example of the use of this imagery in a multi-racial group as a means of releasing feelings about racism and the different perceptions of black and white participants.

Indoor physical activities

Physical movement is itself energising, quite apart from the direct skills and social learning which different kinds of games and indoor activities offer. There is scope for different levels of co-operation and sharing. Physical games are widely used in groupwork with adolescents (Dearling and Armstrong, 1984), but this type of activity also has an important place in adult groups. Dancing, yoga, bioenergetic exercises, or even friendly wrestling may form part of a group programme for adults, who tend to be more inhibited than children about physical interaction and movement. It is often helpful to the members if the worker demonstrates and participates actively, at least in the early stages. It is also part of the worker's responsibility to ensure that the chosen activities are safe physically and within the capabilities of the group members.

Arts and crafts

In social work groups this kind of creative activity is likely to be a therapeutic means to some less tangible end, e.g. drawing and painting may be the most effective means by which some members can communicate with others. For a detailed account of the potential of *art therapy* in groups see Liebmann (1986). Creative art techniques can also be very effective with young children (Clerkin and Knaggs, 1991).

'Outside' activities

This refers to all those activities which necessitate the group moving away physically from its usual base. Included are trips, visits (educational/leisure), outdoor sports and pursuits, camping, community projects and many others. For some groups this will form the major part of their programme, for others it will be a minor but important part designed to provide diversity, perhaps an anticipated high-light such as a boat trip, offering a new context for group experience. The effect can sometimes 'free-up' a group to move forward after a static period. There are likely to be practical problems to cope with such as transport, finance and insurance.

In groupwork, outside activities are usually of value in themselves, but they are also a means to other goals which the group may have such as developing skills in social interaction and increasing an individual's self-confidence. If the activity is, or becomes, the primary goal, then it may have a more appropriate place in educational, industrial training or sports programmes.

Games and simulations

There are many games which groups can play as a different, and often very acceptable, way of interacting and learning. One example is a game designed to help members give each other personal feedback. One person at a time volunteers to be the focus, and all the other group members have to think, silently, of an animal that the person particularly reminds them of. Then, in turn, each member divulges the chosen animal and gives reasons for the resemblance. Another variation is to ask each member to suggest an animal which they think characterises them as they are and another which symbolises how they would like to be. The self-image can then be put alongside the perceptions of others. This is both good fun and a relatively unthreatening way of giving and receiving personal feedback. Several comprehensive collec-tions of group games are now available (see Brandes and Phillips, 1978; Brandes, 1982; Ernst and Goodison, 1982; Johnson and Johnson, 1975). Gaie Houston's two 'Red Books' on *Groups* and *Gestalt* contain a rich and imaginative collection of group exercises which can be used as they stand or adapted to suit the needs of a particular group (Houston, 1990a and 1990b).

Inter-group or inter-role activities

This refers to programmed contacts between a group and either other groups or individuals in particular roles. One example of an inter-group meeting that involved two Family Service Unit parents' groups has already been referred to (Walker, 1978). Bazalgette (1971) programmed groups for school-leavers and others in the 14–21 age range, to meet individual adults who were in community roles carrying authority which had special significance for them, e.g. employer, vicar, policeman, social worker, careers advisory officer. Another group invited the leader of a youth club where some of them had been banned for unruly behaviour. A single-parents' group invited a welfare-rights lawyer to discuss financial and legal problems. The aim of these interchanges may vary from social learning to role-testing to obtaining expert advice to advocacy for social change.

Interactions of this kind can be useful, especially in longer-term groups, but they can also be diversionary or even lead to disruptive competition and hostility. They need therefore to be programmed with caution and skill. The beginning groupworker sometimes experiences a self-generated pressure to involve outside 'experts' to compensate for feelings of personal inadequacy, or fears that the group will not have enough to do. These pressures need to be tested against the likelihood of positive gain. The early forming–storming stages of a new group are not usually a good time to bring in outside influences. These are likely to be coped with better when the group has developed its own strength and cohesion, and perhaps needs a new stimulus.

The above examples are ones in which the groupworker is playing a major role in the group programme. In self-directed groups (Mullender and Ward 1991) and self-help groups with a social action aim, inter-group relations and activities initiated by the group members themselves are likely to be a priority area for participants' skill development.

Relaxation exercises

Many groups, particularly those with members suffering from high levels of mental and/or physical stress, find it useful to include periods of time devoted to relaxation. Starting with facilitated relaxation may be equally helpful, for example, to those with back-pain (one such group started with 20 minutes relaxation) or those with agoraphobia.

Audio-tapes 'leading' relaxation sequences are widely available, and the straightforward method of tensing up and then relaxing all the different parts of the body in turn, is very effective.

Assignments or homework

These have already been referred to as those programme activities which an individual or sub-group agrees to carry out between sessions. The tasks need to be manageable, carrying a high expectation of success, and if possible, fairly specific and easily evaluated by the individual or sub-group.

An example of effective use of group programme

The reader is referred to an excellent account by Ross and Bilson (1981) of the thoughtful and imaginative use of group programme. Their 'Sunshine Group' was a twelve-session intensive group for children of both sexes, aged 9–11, who had experienced sexual abuse as either perpetrator or victim. The workers carefully assessed the need to be met and worked out a flexible programme response which included a whole range of creative play, discussion, games and drama techniques, as well as a three-day residential period after the eighth session.

Some difficulties which can arise in groups and possible ways of resolving them

One of the main reasons for planning and preparing a group very carefully is to reduce the likelihood of serious dysfunctioning occurring, but groupwork is about people interacting together, often under stress, and this inevitably produces some difficulties as well as many benefits. Two of the most common causes of concern and anxiety for groupworkers and group members are: firstly, when individuals get into problematic roles, and secondly, when the whole group takes on a stance which seems to get in the way of group development and task achievement. We shall consider each of these in turn, developing a consistent conceptual framework, selecting a few of the most common examples of each 'problem', and suggesting various strategies which may help the worker, and the group, to resolve the difficulty.

The individual and the group

A group is a dynamic interacting system in which each individual's role and behaviour is in varying degrees a function of the group-as-a-whole and of group process as well as an individual characteristic. As a group develops, the roles get shared around among the members. Sometimes an individual finds a role which enables her both to contribute to, and to benefit from, the group in a way suiting her personal resources and needs. At other times people get 'stuck' in problematic roles which may be dysfunctional for them, and also for the group.

Examples of problematic roles are the 'scapegoat', the 'monopoliser', the 'silent member', the 'deviant', the 'absent member', and the 'disrupter'. In order to understand what is happening (and therefore to begin to have ideas about a solution) a group perspective is needed which, whilst appreciating that an individual often attracts a particular role, recognises that he can also have it reinforced or 'put on him' by others, often unconsciously. Thus, for example, scapegoating is a process in which one group member is isolated and has ascribed to him (negative) feelings, wishes or behaviour which others are unable to recognise or accept in themselves and then attack in the scapegoat. A monopoliser can only dominate a group as long as others tacitly allow her to do so, and a silent member may find himself in that position because others are not open to what he may have to contribute. The basic theoretical assumption is that individual behaviours may often have *group purpose*. They are functional in a process sense for the group, although they may be dysfunctional for task achievement. This has implications for worker response and problem resolution.

We shall now consider a range of possible responses applicable to any problematic individual role behaviour in a group and then comment on the special features of scapegoating, monopolising and being silent.

1) *'Do nothing'*. It is essential that the worker waits a little

while, firstly to tune-in to the dynamic and make sure she understands what is happening, and secondly in the hope that group members may take some initiative themselves in drawing attention to, and helping to resolve, the difficulty. To allow the problem to persist indefinitely, however, is to abdicate the responsibility that is part of being a group-worker.

2)   *Indirect responses.* These are approaches in which the worker tries to influence what is happening without drawing attention to it explicitly or directly. One way of doing this which can be quite effective is through the use of group programme. This means using different group structures, activities or exercises to shift the group balance. One simple structure is 'going round the circle' in which each member has their turn to contribute without having to claim it by 'getting in'. (Many people find a role offered by a structure an easier basis for contributing in a group than when they have to take the risk and the initiative themselves.) Alternatively workers may use seating arrangements, non-verbal communication and various other forms of 'engineering' to reinforce desired changes and free up the problematic role.

3)   *Direct implicit responses.* Some responses can be direct without referring explicitly to the underlying issue. An example of this is making a point of offering a silent member the opportunity to speak, asking a monopoliser to keep quiet while somebody else is contributing, or turning away from the monopoliser and saying 'what do others think?'

4)   *Direct explicit responses.* There are three possibilities here, each making explicit reference to 'the problem':

(a)   *to speak directly to the individual* ('Mary, you seem to be getting blamed for everything that goes wrong in this group', 'Jim, can you tell the rest of us what makes it difficult for you to speak in this group', 'Jean, you talk so much it's difficult to hear the important things you have to say');

(b)   *to speak directly to the rest of the group* ('I think we need to try and understand why you are always having a go at Mary', 'Does it concern the rest of you that Jim is silent and gets ignored', 'The rest of you are letting Jean do nearly all the talking in this group'); or

(c) *to address the group-as-a-whole* ('I suggest we stop
what we're doing for a few minutes because we're not
working together very well as a group at the moment
... I'm sure we've all noticed that ... Let's try and
find out what everyone in the group thinks about
what's been happening and see if we can agree a way of
working together which will be better for everyone
...).

Of these three 'explicit' options, the first two will, on
occasion, be appropriate/necessary but they both have the
basic flaw (as a starting point) of reinforcing the split
between the individual and the group. The third option of
addressing the group-as-a-whole is generally to be preferred
because it reinforces the basic premise of shared responsibility for what happens in the group. It takes a bit of courage
for the worker to be direct and explicit about the difficulty,
and initially the intervention may be met by denial or
hostility, but there is likely also to be considerable relief in
the group that something everyone was aware of can now be
talked about. The worker's aim is for a resolution which
both frees the individual from the unhelpful role and enables
the whole group to move forward with the task. This process
often includes the facilitation of feedback between members
about how they are experiencing each other's behaviour.

The worker herself is powerfully affected by the group
dynamic and this can sometimes lead her to protect (the
scapegoat, silent member) or attack (the monopoliser, the
scapegoaters) which is unlikely to benefit the individual or
the group except in extreme circumstances where, for
example, the physical protection of an individual or the
removal of a severe disrupter may be necessary. Consultation can be particularly effective in enabling a worker to
disentangle her personal feelings sufficiently to facilitate
productive change in the group.

5) *Contact outside the group.* Another possible response is
to make contact with the individual member outside the
group. This approach is to be used selectively and sensitively
depending on (a) the urgency of the individual need and the
availability or otherwise of alternative sources of support/
contact, and (b) the extent to which the individual contact is
likely to facilitate a group resolution of the problem. What is

to be avoided is getting into a special relationship with one group member outside the group which includes discussion of their relationship with other members in the group. Group business needs to be resolved within the group.

The 'monopoliser'.   The monopoliser may be useful to the group in the early stages of uncertainty and dependency but as time passes he becomes not only increasingly resented by other members, but also a threat to the position of the worker. It is nearly always necessary to take action with a persistent monopoliser because there can be serious repercussions among the other members who, if the worker does not take an initiative, may be deterred from returning to the group. The important thing to hold on to (as you struggle to manage your own strong feelings!) is that frequently beneath the monopoliser's stream of verbiage that person has something important to express and contribute to the group. Exceptionally a monopoliser may be so destructive that the last resort of exclusion from the group is necessary.

The 'scapegoat'.   The scapegoat is unlikely or unwilling to defend herself effectively or to do much about it. This suggests that the role is in some way functional and satisfying for her as well as for the group. Negative attention may be preferred to no attention. Typically, groups ostracise, institutionalise or encapsulate scapegoats. The more institutionalised the role becomes in the group the harder it is to relinquish it because it fits everyone's expectations. The worker often feels drawn to protect the scapegoat and to reverse the blame to the rest of the group, or particular 'persecutory' individuals. Even without this, the mere exposure of the scapegoating phenomenon in the group is often unpopular (because it faces others with *their* 'nasty' bits) and it is not uncommon for the worker to get scapegoated instead – be prepared!

Garland and Kolodny (1972), much of whose work was with adolescents, listed the following range of techniques to counteract scapegoating:

(a)   *Direct squashing*: 'This taunting of John has got to stop or else . . .' This threatening approach is not recommended.

(b) *Giving information* (about an individual): 'John had a bladder operation which makes it difficult for him to stop wetting his pants.' This raises ethical questions about confidentiality, and is generally not recommended.

(c) *Protection*: intervening physically or verbally to restrain attackers. This will on occasion be necessary to protect the individual, but can have the consequence of reinforcing rather than alleviating the scapegoating.

(d) *Diversion*: picking another target, perhaps the worker himself, or changing activities to ones that John is better at than some of the other group members.

(e) *Reducing interaction*: structuring activities, perhaps in sub-groups, to minimise contagion; or arranging a break (an under-used technique which can be a very effective way of changing the climate in a group).

(f) *Ego-support*: particularly for *other* group members who may then feel secure enough to contain their own feelings and aggression.

(g) *Clarification/direct comment*: 'John seems to be getting a lot of stick today.' This can open up, or legitimise, direct explicit discussion of the group behaviour.

(h) *Allowing scapegoating to flower*: bringing the behaviour into sharp and obvious focus, attempting change by the 'paradox' of highlighting rather than disguising defence mechanisms. This requires a high level of skill and experience.

(i) *Helping the group to control the scapegoating behaviour*: this can often be effective, drawing on group strengths, particularly when the scapegoat is not too isolated.

(j) *Playing out the scapegoat process*: for example through the use of role-play or sociodrama techniques, which can release feelings and increase understanding, producing conditions for change in the group.

(k) *Removal of the scapegoat*: this is very much a last resort if the evidence suggests that the group is incapable of resolving the scapegoating and continuation in the group will be destructive for the person scapegoated. Another 'last ditch' option is of course to terminate the whole group.

The choice of techniques from this range, within the framework outlined at the beginning of this section, will depend on the particular group stage and circumstances, an assessment of group process and strengths, the style and intuition of the groupworker, and what is likely to be effective.

The 'silent member'.   I personally find this one of the most difficult situations to know how to respond to helpfully. I think there are two reasons for this. The personal reason is that I rarely find myself in this position in small groups and therefore am not always as understanding or sensitive as I ought to be! The more general reason is that silent members do not intrude on group business and other members in such an obvious way, and it is sometimes difficult to judge why they are quiet and whether they wish to remain silent or to be helped to participate. A member may take on a silent role for a variety of reasons, such as fear of self-disclosure, lack of assertiveness, self-protection against vulnerability, fear of losing control, or to cope with a perceived threat from one or more others in the group. Experience suggests that people who are habitually quiet in groups would usually like to be helped to be more (verbally) active, but without being put on the spot.

Structured opportunities or quiet encouragement are appreciated. Shulman (1984) suggests that the worker speaks with the quiet member outside the group and makes a secret arrangement about signals in the group. As stated earlier, I think contact outside the group does have a place as another strategy in the resolution of these individual behaviours, particularly when it really does seem to be more an individual than a group problem. However in general I prefer in-group methods without special alliances or secrets between worker and member, as these can further isolate that member within the group.

Shulman (1984) has a good section on 'the individual and the group' and Yalom (1975) and Whitaker (1985) also cover this topic comprehensively. Garland and Kolodny (1972) and Anstey (1982) give special attention to scapegoating. Douglas (1991) has recently produced a handbook on *Common Groupwork Problems*.

Whole-group 'problems'

Every groupworker will have experienced times when the whole group takes on a particular characteristic which appears to be impeding progress. The group may go silent, apathetic, resistant, attacking, depressed, jokey. The first thing, as a worker, is to manage your own feelings about what is happening – there is usually an important message if you are able to listen and not just feel frustrated, angry, depressed or impotent. The range of possible responses is similar to that suggested above for problematic individual roles, but the focus of interest is much more likely to be the worker–group relationship and the issue of authority, particularly in the early stages of a group. Shulman (1984) has pointed out that the members have to deal with the worker's ability to control, to make demands and to care, as well as coping with her or his limitations and her or his role as 'outsider' in the group. A second area which may be contributing to group problems is intimacy and the relationship between members.

I never cease to be amazed at how different the mood of the same group can be from one session to the next, which indicates the wisdom of 'hanging in there' before reacting too swiftly. When the time does come to act, the response may be direct or indirect, implicit or explicit. As a general guideline, observation and comments on what is going on are more positively received than 'clever' interpretations or apparent criticisms of the members. Explicit use of what *you* are feeling can be helpful, and risk-taking often produces positive results.

For example, a group of offenders in an 'alcohol discussion group' were expected to share with the others their past drinking behaviour, in response to questioning in the 'hot seat'. Nobody volunteered and the atmosphere got very sticky. Ultimately one of the two workers agreed to take the hot-seat himself; the group's energy visibly returned and he was subjected to questioning firstly by his co-worker and then by other group members. After a while a group member volunteered to take the hot-seat and the impasse was broken. One potential trap in this resolution is the worker getting caught in a member role and being used vicariously by members, thus perpetuating risk-avoidance rather than role-modelling risk-taking in a way they then can follow. Having a co-worker can be most helpful in this type of situation because she can 'manage' the episode and hold on to the worker–member boundary, helping her colleague to do likewise.

For further discussion about the ways in which different kinds of group culture and structures develop, and ways in which workers can facilitate group development and 'enabling solutions' see Heap (1985), Shulman (1984), Whitaker (1985) and Douglas (1991). Heap (Chapter 6) has a particularly useful section which explores the different reasons for 'group silences' and he suggests a range of different 'matched' responses by the worker.

Final comment on difficulties

When approaching individual and group difficulties it is always necessary to remember that some individuals can be very vulnerable in groups and are potential casualties (see Galinsky and Schopler, 1977). They may, for example, lose control of themselves, sob violently or behave in a way likely to damage themselves or others. They may become depressed and withdrawn. If their vulnerability is predominantly a personal matter, then maximum support should be offered to the individual within and outside the group (in extreme cases they may need to withdraw from the group). If however the vulnerability is a group-induced phenomenon of the kind discussed in this section, then it is group business to work it out together, with the aim of individuals owning their own agendas instead of depositing them on others.

5 Working with Groups in Day and Residential Centres

The other chapters in this book outline an approach to groupwork which covers many of the concepts and skills needed when undertaking groupwork in a fieldwork setting. These groups typically meet once a week, or perhaps every two weeks, and the workers and the members often may not have any contact at all with each other between group sessions. Contrast this with what happens in day and residential centres! Here the pattern is completely different because workers and members share together in group living. In the course of one day – and perhaps night – there is a mixture of many different kinds of group encounters, varying from casual groupings around a coffee bar to organised groups for specific purposes like social skills training. This poses for members and workers alike the 'problem' of how to cope with all these different ways of meeting together, how to adjust from one kind of group to another, and how to keep tabs on what is happening all over the place at the same time. This chapter is designed to provide a framework to help workers in these settings think about the specific group issues which they face. A typology will be outlined of the different kinds of groups and groupings that can be found in these contexts, and we shall consider some of the particular skills which are needed and which differ in some important respects from those suitable for once-a-week fieldwork groups.

Although the term 'group care' is often used to describe residential work, most of the books on the subject do not discuss the group dimension except when talking about the staff group (see for example Atherton, 1986). Much of this chapter is based on the ideas in a book edited by Brown and Clough (1989), which has very detailed practice accounts drawn from different settings and written by people who worked in them. There are examples of work in residential centres for older people, offenders, and people with learning difficulties; and in day centres for families, young people and those with mental health difficulties; and a special kind of family group which takes in children in care on a permanent basis. Readers in search of detailed practical examples are encouraged to refer to that book. Another useful book for thinking more generally about the application of group processes to group living has been written by Douglas (1986). Relevant articles in the journal *Groupwork* include Craig (1988), Bernard *et al.* (1988) and Clarke and Aimable (1990).

Another issue when thinking about working with groups in day and residential centres is the great variation in the types of centre, function and user. The spectrum ranges from residential *homes* which are just that, the permanent homes of people who, because of frailty, physical or mental disability, will live there for the rest of their lives, to drop-in centres which someone may visit for one morning on only one occasion. Readers will therefore have to adapt what follows to the circumstances of the type of centre in which they are particularly interested, and also to the increasingly common 'unstaffed' centres (see Atkinson, 1989). However, I shall be concentrating on those centres where people spend much of their daily living whether or not they are actually resident. This focus is because the group living factor is the one which most distinguishes group practice in centres from mainstream social groupwork. Some of the most important distinguishing features will now be considered.

Features of residential and day centres

Note: It is not possible here to do more than point to some key features of group living which particularly influence the way people relate to one another in groups. Readers wishing to study residential group living in more depth are referred to Clough (1981, 1982) and Fulcher and Ainsworth (1985); and to Carter (1988) for insight into daily life in a day centre for people with learning difficulties.

A physical base

Centres provide a physical location which people visit, or live in, and with which they often feel some identification and belonging. For example, almost all centres have some sort of kitchen, however basic, which may serve as a focal point for people to gather 'just like home'. The provision of a base can itself be therapeutic, for example a women's aid refuge, a children's day nursery, or a residential hostel for people recovering from mental illness. Interaction in a base is much more complex than in a fieldwork group because staff and members will be encountering one another in many different ways, each affecting the others.

The mix of organised and informal groupings

In a centre much that happens is informal and outside any organised programme which may have been arranged. This means among other things that people are having to adjust constantly to new circumstances requiring different kinds of behaviour. For example, in a probation hostel a member of staff may one minute be teaching residents about alcohol abuse in an alcohol education group, later enjoying a meal together perhaps discussing the latest political situation, and much later having to confront an informal group who have been out late together and return to the hostel noisy and much the worse for drink. In a residential home for people suffering from dementia, a worker may one minute be facilitating a reminiscence group, and the next wiping one of the group member's bottoms in the lavatory. This creates a multiplicity of role-relationships and associated feelings not experienced to the same degree in fieldwork.

The self-exposure of users and staff

Groupwork is in general a more personally exposing method of social work than individual casework. This is because in a group there is likely to be a greater degree of equality between workers and users, and an expectation that the workers will join with members in some of the personal sharing and disclosure. Much of the control is held by the group compared to the individual control exerted by the worker in her often powerful position in the one-to-one casework relationship. However in a once-a-week group the worker can if she wishes confine herself to only limited self-exposure. Most of us can be on our best behaviour for an hour and a half, but how many of us can keep it up day in and day out in a group living context?! One consequence of this is that both staff and members are likely to be unconsciously if not consciously sharing much more of themselves in group encounters in centres.

The range of opportunities

One major advantage of the group living features already described is the many and diverse opportunities for people in the centre to meet together. In a once-a-week group, if something difficult or traumatic occurs near the end of a group meeting, members may have to disperse soon afterwards without an opportunity to resolve or heal the difficulty. In a centre everyone knows that there will be many other opportunities during the rest of that day, and in the following days, to work at resolving whatever occurred. The other side of this coin is that risk-taking may feel safer in the confidential temporary context of a fieldwork group than it does in the 'hothouse' atmosphere of group living, where personal privacy may be at a premium. This is why the creation of a facilitating group environment is so essential, a point to which I return in the section on skills.

These important factors, and many others, require a framework for thinking about all these different kinds of groups, the connections between them, and the particular group skills needed by workers in group living settings. The rest of this chapter attempts to provide such a framework, but we need to start by recognising that because so many of the ways in which people meet in residential and day centres are in casual or 'untidy' gatherings we need a different word from 'group'. Following Brown and Clough (1989) we shall use the term 'grouping', which is explained in the next section.

The concept of 'grouping'

The term group tends to be used very loosely to cover virtually any kind of gathering of three or more people however temporary and tenuous. Yet when we talk about groupwork we are thinking of an entity which initially has particular properties like a discernible membership, an aim and a structure; and which develops patterns of group interaction, interdependence and predictable ways of behaving and conducting its business. Many 'groups' in centres are not at all like that. They may be no more than what are called 'aggregates', a term used to describe a collection of people who just happen to be in the same place at the same time, and have no significant patterns of interaction: for example a few people temporarily sitting in the same railway compartment. What is more likely in centres is that people who are together in the same place are having some form of interaction, whether or not they are actually speaking to each other. Often this will be unorganised and temporary without obvious indications of group cohesion. Lang (1986), in a very useful clarification of these issues, refers to this type of gathering as a 'collectivity'. I shall use the term 'grouping'.

Examples of people in groupings in day and residential centres are: people sitting together at mealtimes; people in a minibus on a day trip; spontaneous gatherings for friendship; sharing the same educational class (where group interaction is not a strong feature); watching TV together; temporary gatherings in a 'drop-in' centre; attendances at large meetings for special purposes; and people who tend to be around in the same place at the same time fairly regularly, for example the first arrivals at a mental health day centre having a coffee together, older people in a residential home sitting around in the same chairs in the same room, youngsters meeting together under a favourite tree in the evening, and so on. It can be seen from these examples that the term 'groupings' covers a wide range of different kinds of gathering, some of which may be little more than an aggregate, others of which may develop eventually into cohesive groups. The important point is that in all these instances the roles, functions and skills of the workers (as well as the users) are different, to a greater or lesser extent, from those defined for the 'classical' social groupworker, who is written about in most of the groupwork literature. Yet, the complexity and shifting patterns of groupings and ways of relating in a centre require a quality of 'group' understanding, role-taking and skills at least equal to, perhaps greater than, those expected of a field group-worker. Before we go on to consider what these skills are we need to have a basis for thinking about all the different kinds of groups and groupings which may be found in centres.

A classification of groups and groupings

Brown and Clough (1989) have suggested the following way of distinguishing the different kinds of gatherings which may occur in day and residential centres. The main differentiating factors taken into account are purpose, membership, roles, type of interaction and context. The categories used inevitably overlap due to the dynamic changing nature of centre life.

The whole community

This refers to the total membership of staff and users at the centre. In some places people will have little idea of being part of such a totality, but, nevertheless, the whole community exists. In other establishments there will be a feeling of shared identity, sometimes indicated by the existence of a definite community culture and values, or in a more tangible way by everyone (staff and users) meeting together in regular community meetings which convey a real sense of being part of a single large group or grouping.

Living together 'groups'

These are the groups and groupings in which people are together because they share a group living context which for some is 'home'. Examples include mealtime groups, bed-room groups and people who just like sitting around together in the same room. The appropriate placing on the aggregate . . . grouping . . . group continuum will vary according to the nature of each centre, and how shared living is organised. For example, in centres for very small numbers of people, as in some children's homes, there will be a single living together group.

Informal friendship/affinity groups

These are groupings of people who affiliate together 'natur-ally' when they are not grouped together by others or by set programmes. The reasons for their affinity may stem from some shared characteristic, common interest, spontaneous friendship and many other factors. They are different from many of the other groups and groupings because *they* (the members) have chosen whom they want to be with – or been chosen or pressured by their peers!

Groups to discuss group living issues

These groups are for staff and/or users. They may be called house meetings, tenants' meetings, centre meetings, group meetings, or any other title. Their purpose is to discuss matters of shared concern arising from group living, whether residential or non-residential. Examples of agenda items might be: meals, money, rules, membership, sanctions, responsibilities, activities, centre events and other matters arising from shared living.

Organised groups

These are groups similar in format and purpose to formed groups in fieldwork settings. They will have some stability of membership, will give attention to group interaction and process, and will focus on issues relevant to members' lives outside the centre (or inside the centre if it is their long-term home). These kinds of groups include therapy, counselling, skill development, activities, behaviour change, problem-solving, personal growth, empowerment and social action; as well as groups for specific needs or difficulties, e.g. reminiscence, assertiveness, substance abuse, bereavement.

Organised groupings

These groupings occur because people come together for some activity, for example educational classes, clubs, music, games, domestic tasks and other regular centre activities. Unlike the previous category of organised groups, these groupings may not give much attention to interaction between members, group cohesion, mutual aid and other group characteristics.

These groupings for activities will often be initiated and

organised by staff, but in some centres some activities will be initiated by users (or jointly) and may include for example, running a shop, providing coffee, organising an event, representing the user group on various committees, forming a pressure group to obtain resources, negotiating with staff.

Groupings for special 'one off' events are a further variation. These fall into two broad categories:

(a)   *Inside* the establishment. For example: plays, assemblies, parties, visiting speakers or entertainers, religious services.

(b)   *Outside* the establishment. For example: outings, trips, expeditions, camps, educational visits.

Staff groups and groupings

These are of three main types. The first are formal groups like staff meetings for running and managing the centre: the size and number of these will vary according to the size of the centre and how it is organised. The second are groupings of staff responsible for particular activities like the many different kinds already referred to. The third are the informal, self-generated affinity sub-groupings of staff which may be based on shared characteristics such as age, race, gender and roles; shared values, attitudes and political views; or the mutual attraction of people who like being together.

Groups and groupings whose membership crosses the boundary of the centre

Examples of these kinds of groups, which contain both 'insiders' and 'outsiders', are family groups, case conferences, teams of field and day/residential staff, and groups including both residents/users and members of the local community. The groups may be formal or informal, and a significant factor will be whether they are held on the centre premises or on some other territory. *'Drop-in' groupings*, which do not fit neatly into any of the above categories, can be considered as falling into this category because there is by definition no restriction on membership and they are often intended to bridge the boundary between the centre and the community. Mention should also be made of groups which are entirely composed of 'outsiders', perhaps a local club of some kind, but which meet on the premises of the centre.

One particular centre may not have all of these different kinds of groups and groupings, but many will have what are, from the viewpoint of a new user (or indeed a new staff member), a bewildering array of contexts to cope with in a day and a week. The user in a centre has to learn how to adapt to a series of encounters in groups and groupings which will not necesarily be ones that they would have chosen: for example, who they sit next to at the meal table, and in the TV room. Thus boundary-crossing and 'managing transitions' emerge as crucial features of group living – something I shall return to later.

Principles and values

The importance of the *external environment* as a major influence on the success or otherwise of a group has already been discussed and underlined in earlier chapters. This applies at two levels in a group living centre. Firstly, all that happens inside the centre will be affected by both the policy of the managing agency, and the attitude of people in the immediate neighbourhood in which it is physically located. An example of the former is the agency staffing policy, and of the latter is the friendly support or outright hostility of neighbours to, say, a new 'house' for people recovering from mental illness. These external factors will not be discussed further here, but the reader is encouraged to look at Burton's fascinating case-study of the possibilities of intro- ducing fundamental change into a traditional 'old people's home', notwithstanding an unsympathetic agency policy (Burton, 1989).

Secondly, the *internal climate* of a centre will profoundly affect every group and grouping that meets there. This underlines the importance of having some agreed general principles and values which prevail throughout the centre, thus providing a consistent framework for all the different activities and interactions. These will now be considered in more detail.

In a fieldwork setting it is possible, though probably not

desirable, to carry out a range of discrete tasks in very different, even contradictory, ways and 'get away with it'. In a group living centre everything is much more inter-related, so that if there are major inconsistencies in approach to different events this will immediately face staff and users with much uncertainty and confusion. For example, if in one particular group a staff member challenges a sexist or racist remark, and then users observe other staff members not only not challenging but actively colluding with racist or sexist behaviour this is likely to create instability and divisions which undermine the successful achievement of centre objectives for users. For these reasons, it is necessary to have some agreed principles which will apply to all gatherings and interaction. These principles often take a long hard struggle to agree and establish. Ball and Sowa (1989, page 140) give an interesting illustration in their account of groupwork in an intermediate treatment centre. The issue was whether staff should be allowed to take underage young people to the pub occasionally. After debate a groundrule was established that this was not acceptable, and the minority of staff who disagreed accepted the decision in the interests of presenting the young people with a consistent policy. In a family centre (Stones, 1989) staff faced another problem. They were agreed among themselves on an anti-racist policy, but many of their white, mostly female working-class users who they were seeking to empower disagreed. How could they reconcile two apparently contradictory principles?

Brown and Clough (1989), drawing on the experience and comments of leading practitioners who contributed to their text, suggest four general principles for group living which if adopted would apply to all the groups and groupings in a centre. The four are: *empowering users*; *equality of rights and opportunities*; *partnership*; and *seeing things from the user's perspective*. These principles are of course merely rhetoric unless they are translated into specific groundrules governing how people relate together. The advantage of establishing a shared framework known to all staff and users is that it provides a common yardstick for responding to issues in whatever group context they may arise in a centre.

Another general principle which if applied will greatly enhance the likelihood of positive group experiences is *the establishment of a facilitative culture and climate*. In order to achieve this kind of culture certain conditions need to prevail. Some of the most important will now be considered.

Firstly, the importance of the physical environment of the centre as a whole and of the different places in which groups and groupings meet cannot be overestimated. People feel more valued when trouble has been taken to make 'their' territory attractive and conducive to working/playing productively together.

Secondly, it can be helpful if there are some occasions when everyone in a centre meets together, thus demonstrating visually and experientially that they are all part of a community. However, large groups can be frightening places, and it will be important to plan very carefully to ensure that everyone feels they belong and can have a part in it, even if this is indirectly through another who speaks for them perhaps through presenting an agreed proposal.

Thirdly, it is important that the 'outer-boundary' of the centre is managed in a way congruent with its objectives. If the centre is the permanent home of the residents, then as far as possible they are entitled to the degree of privacy that they would enjoy in a home of their own. If it is a community-based family centre with a drop-in group open to the whole neighbourhood, then it is essential that it is equally welcoming to men and women, black and white, older and younger people.

The fourth facilitating factor will be the establishment of groundrules, as indicated above, providing a basis for living and working together. These are likely to be much more effective if they have been negotiated and agreed with users and not imposed, although in some circumstances on some issues that may be necessary.

Fifthly, it goes almost without saying that the attitudes and behaviour of staff, with each other and with users, will set the tone for the whole place and all that happens whether in formal groups or informal gatherings. In residential and day centre work, staff are consciously or unconsciously modelling for users ways of relating and treating each other. A key aspect in this will be the composition of the staff group and perhaps most important of all the style and approach of the person in charge, who is the most powerful role-model of all. A manager who preaches empowerment of users and proceeds to disempower her staff colleagues will not be very convincing!

A repertoire of group skills for group living

What group skills do day and residential staff need in addition to those necessary when working with groups in fieldwork settings? Skills involve thinking and understanding as well as doing, so the worker first needs to have a clear idea of the context in which he or she is working. One way of conceptualising this is to view the centre as operating at three levels:

(1) *the centre-as-a-whole*, that is the totality of everything that is happening in the centre;
(2) *the mosaic of interacting parts*, each part in relation to the whole, and vice versa;
(3) *the discrete single groups and groupings*.

Specific skills are needed at each of these levels, the common factor being that whatever is done in any one of these spheres of activity has to be undertaken with an eye on the effect of, and the effect on, the others.

Staff skills in the role of group member

Every worker in a day or residential centre needs good skills in functioning as a team member. There is nothing more incongruous than aspiring groupworkers who seem unable to function effectively as group members in their own staff group! In fieldwork this is problematic, but in group living contexts it is even more serious because, as mentioned earlier, staff relationships are much more visible to users. This does not mean that staff have to behave as paragons of virtue, but it does mean that their group and individual behaviour will not only be observed by users, but quite possibly will actually be mirrored by them. What staff demonstrate in their work relationships with each other, for example about coping with authority, managing conflict, intimacy, confidentiality, stress and changes of membership, will be experienced and observed by everyone in the centre.

Some would go so far as to say that when difficulties are occurring in the user group the first place to look for a possible explanation is in the dynamics of the staff group!

The skills needed are thus all those learned for working effectively with users in groups. They include: task and process skills; skills in developing group cohesion and trust; skills in enabling each member to contribute to the best of their ability; skills in confronting and challenging in ways that do not diminish the other person; and so on. However, these are not all skills to be developed by the individual staff member alone and then 'applied' in the staff group: many of them are group functioning skills for the staff group as a unit to develop. This is not easy, and often has to be worked at hard by the staff as a unit over a period of time, perhaps on 'away-days', and if necessary with an outside consultant.

Working with large groups and groupings

Some centres, for example therapeutic communities, have frequent large group gatherings of all the staff and users in the centre. These meetings may be called 'community meetings'. We know from our own experience, and from those who have studied large group behaviour (see Kreeger, 1975), that these kinds of large gatherings can be very difficult and sometimes frightening occasions. We also know that they can be very inspiring and empowering occasions, when they are managed well and with careful preparation. The difficulties arise because, unlike small groups, it is impossible to have eye contact and a feeling of being in touch with all the other members simultaneously. Worse still, it is easy to have the feeling of being alone and isolated from everyone else, whether you are silent or take the risk of saying something. This is partly because in large groups there is not usually the opportunity for early feedback and checking out the reactions of others to what you say, as there is in small groups.

People in groups need to feel they belong, and to achieve this in a large group needs much more structure and planning than in a small group with its 'natural' feeling of intimacy. Staff, and those members who are able, need to take steps both before and during the meeting to try and ensure that every individual can relate to an understandable structure, with facilitated opportunities to participate in the process. The chairing may be shared with members, clear rules may need to be established to ensure that everyone who wants to speak can do so, and periods in small groups or pairs can be used to make sure that everyone can feel related to others. Meetings need to be organised so that each individual's views can feed into the large group discussion whether or not that person is able to speak for themself. If it is a formal kind of meeting, people need to know how they can get items on the agenda and how decisions will be taken. One of the things we know from research on group size is that as groups get larger and larger so fewer and fewer individuals will speak more and more. Conversely, the quieter, less confident people become increasingly silenced. This familiar phenomenon can of course be counteracted to some extent by the kind of careful, enabling thinking and planning that I am advocating.

Inter-group skills and 'helicoptering'

In centres both users and staff will have membership of a range of groups and groupings. This requires special skills in coping with the different tasks and memberships of each gathering, as well as skill in having to adapt quite frequently from one milieu to another. This presents the worker with a double challenge: first to develop the appropriate skills herself, and secondly to enable users to develop the skills they need. An understanding of what we have learned from studies of inter-group relations may be helpful (see for example Levinson and Astrachan,1976).

These studies show, and again our own experience will confirm, that left to their own devices relations between small groups are often characterised by irrational as well as rational feelings which can include: rivalry, splitting (our group is good, yours is bad), envy, superiority, inferiority, comparison, competitiveness and so on. If one group or grouping has more power than another, for example staff *vis-à-vis* users, this is likely to exacerbate and distort inter-group relations further. Another complication will be 'cross-membership' of several groupings leading to potential role-conflict. For example, a user may find it quite confusing to be confronting staff one minute in a staff/users house meeting, having lunch with them the next, and perhaps later that day in a women's group sharing with a female member of staff the common experience of being subjected to male sexism and harassment.

A core skill to help with these dynamics is developing a centre climate and ethos in which differences between individuals and groups are valued and respected, and seen as enriching rather than divisive. That alone will not be sufficient to counteract the tendency to polarise both group-ings and individuals. The task for the worker is firstly to avoid collusion (like the seduction of being told that you are the most understanding staff member or the best group leader!, or the unwitting reinforcement of a comment that the carpentry group is for those who are 'thick'), and secondly to intervene in ways which validate rather than denigrate other people, activities and groupings in the centre.

Hawkins (1989) has coined the useful analogy of 'helicop-tering' to convey the skill that a centre worker needs to enable her or him to be simultaneously deeply involved in some part of a centre and its life, whilst still having an awareness of what is going on elsewhere in the establish-ment. This is a skill that cannot easily be taught or trained for, as it is akin to having the 'sixth sense' which often comes only with experience. Where theory can help is in appreciating the systemic connectedness of the part with the whole.

Boundaries and the management of transitions

Given the different characteristics of the various groups and groupings in the same centre, and the inter-group dynamics which tend to polarise these differences, the actual process of moving out of one group into another assumes crucial importance. It is easy enough to plan that at 11 am Mary goes from a house meeting to a counselling group, or that John goes from art therapy to a sports activity, but for the individual each move may require adaptations of place, purpose, atmosphere, membership and staffing. Feelings do not fit easily into compartments, and as the individual enters the next grouping, she may still be carrying strong feelings about what she has just experienced. An example of this can be seen in social work education where the college institution has many of the characteristics of a day centre. Lecturers have been known to move straight into, say, a seminar on housing policy quite oblivious of the fact that the students are very churned up physically and emotionally, having just come from watching some slides of the different kinds of injuries that can be inflicted in child abuse.

The staff skills required to facilitate these transitions are both in planning programmes sensitively to take account of the transitions people will have to make (including having appropriate spaces between commitments for debriefing), and in the ways members are helped both to leave one group and to enter the next. The ending skills discussed in Chapter 4 are not just for when a whole group programme ends, but apply equally to the ending of each meeting or activity, especially when the group members are about to move on to a different grouping and type of participation. This means, for example, making sure there is time to complete any outstanding 'business', particularly if it is contentious or unfinished.

Similarly, group forming skills are needed at the beginning of every new grouping, for example allowing time at the start to allow people to reform, and if necessary to express and share feelings or preoccupations which they may have brought with them from the previous experience. Paradoxically, an opportunity to share the 'baggage' from a previous experience at the beginning of a new one can free up someone to give their attention to the new event and expectations. This has to be done in a way which acknowledges but does not perpetuate what is brought in from elsewhere. There may however sometimes be occasions when members and/or staff decide to abandon the planned purpose for the new group and concentrate on 'processing' what is brought in because it is so strong and pervasive. For example members may just have heard that a valued staff member is leaving, or someone in the centre has a serious illness. At its best a group living context offers the flexibility to be responsive to preoccupations in the here-and-now, wherever or whatever that group context might be.

Small group skills

Many centres include in their programme small groups which are similar in format to those organised in fieldwork settings. Examples of these might be a reminiscence group for older people, a parenting skills group, a psychodrama group or a welfare rights group. The worker with responsibility for facilitating such a group in a centre needs all the skills appropriate in the fieldwork setting *plus* additional ones which take account of the group living context of the group.

We have already referred to the work to be done at the beginning and the end of a meeting to facilitate transfer between different activities and experiences. The worker also needs to behave in ways which are congruent with the ethos of the centre and any agreed groundrules, for example on racism and other forms of violence. Another difference from a once-a-week fieldwork group is the additional choice open to the group members and the workers about when and where to take on issues which arise. For example, someone in a small group may be getting scapegoated by other group members. In the fieldwork context the worker may decide that the difficulty has to be dealt with there and then in the meeting in which it occurs because the only alternative is to do nothing for a week, with the risk of it festering and the individual not returning to the group. In a centre there will be many other opportunities in the hours following the incident, both informally and in other groupings, presenting the workers with a choice about which context is likely to be most conducive to a good resolution of the difficulty.

This flexibility requires close understanding and continuous communication between staff about their approach to group relationship issues. Without this a situation could develop where either no one addressed the issue or several all tried without awareness of what others were doing or of the collective impact on the individual and other group members. The foregoing should not be taken to imply that the responsibility for 'sorting out problems' lies exclusively with the staff. Users who are encouraged to take responsibility can develop very sensitive awareness about these issues and may well be better judges than staff about how to make the best possible use of the choice of approach and context for dealing with interpersonal issues.

Working with groupings

We shall now explore the particular skills that apply when working with groupings. It would be difficult, and indeed inappropriate, to generalise when groupings have been defined as including a whole range of gatherings of quite different kinds, their only common feature being that they do not have all the properties associated with developed groups. Another important distinction which we shall return to is between groupings which are initiated by staff and those which are initiated by users.

When considering worker skills in any group context, being clear about the role of the worker and his or her relationship with the members individually and collectively is paramount. The groupwork concept of the worker as 'central person' is helpful here. In Chapter 3 on leadership we noted that in mainstream models of social groupwork the worker is often viewed as adopting, and being placed in, the central role at the beginning, and then as the group develops an ethos of collective responsibility, so the worker moves to a more peripheral role. In the latter stages, depending on the type of group, the worker will either revert to a more central position to help the group manage ending, or alternatively hand over the entire responsibility to the members as in a self-help group. We also referred to Heap's (1988) distinction between situational and emotional centrality, the former deriving from agency role, structure and resources, the latter being more to do with values and the psychological significance of the worker for the members. Heap's point, that whilst it is nearly always appropriate for the worker to shed the situational centrality as the group progresses, often the emotional centrality stays because the members themselves need it that way, is particularly relevant and important when considering group living contexts. Here the worker often carries strong psychological significance for users because so much time is spent in each other's company and the staff are often in a very powerful position in users' lives. Thus in centres there may be many groupings where the worker is not present physically but is very much present emotionally and psychologically.

One set of gatherings which are being called groupings are those which are not groups because they are too large, temporary, highly structured or didactic for much group interaction to occur. In these circumstances I would agree with Sulman (1986) that it may sometimes be appropriate for the worker to retain the central role throughout. Examples could include an art class in a day centre or a large monthly ward meeting in a psychiatric hospital – although some of these latter occasions might well benefit from a decrease in the central power wielded by the consultant and an increase in patient power.

Another type of gathering in centres is those self-generated groupings which occur spontaneously such as affinity groupings. In these instances, and bearing in mind the point about the emotional significance of staff *in absentia*, the worker has to develop skills in judging when to link with a grouping, for example 'having a chat' as you happen to pass by, and when not to get involved. With good communication, verbal and non-verbal, the experienced sensitive worker is able to pick up the signs from users indicating whether or not they would like her involvement with their grouping. The members' wishes are not of course the only criterion. On the one hand the staff may be trying to reduce the dependency of users, and this could indicate not being easily available or only getting involved temporarily and non-centrally. Alternatively there could be circumstances where the grouping is thought to be potentially destructive and a degree of imposition of staff presence may be judged necessary. Examples of this might be criminal sub-groupings in a probation hostel, groupings of bullies in a children's home or racist and sexist groupings in any setting where the power of some is being used to demean and persecute others. In these circumstances the worker may need to impose herself on a grouping in the wider interests of the centre and maintaining agreed values. This could be considered as legitimate use of situational and emotional centrality.

It is important to remember that in any situation where people are grouped together, interactions with any one individual have significance for others in the grouping. For example the behaviour of a staff member sitting at the meal table with a few residents will be thoroughly scrutinised, whether or not consciously. If the staff person gets very involved with one particular individual, necessary as this may be, the others may well feel excluded in some way. The skill lies in the use of eye contact and other forms of communication with the other people in the grouping to indicate awareness of their existence and importance. This can then be reinforced by the staff person engaging directly with the others subsequently so they have space for their concerns. This kind of group awareness and sharing of attention which is of obvious and basic importance in conventional groupwork is likely to be just as important when being with people in unstructured groupings. One of the indicators of the skilled experienced worker in group living centres, is the capacity to appear quite informal and spontaneous in loose groupings with users, say on an outing or when watching television, whilst at the same time interacting in a way which takes account of both individual and collective needs and the aims of the service being provided.

Use of self

A final point to stress in this consideration of work with groups and groupings in day and residential centres is the core skill of use of self. In these settings workers and users alike are much more accessible and much more vulnerable than in a fieldwork context. This carries many potential advantages and corresponding risks. Social work consumer research in fieldwork settings (for example Sainsbury, 1975; C. Brown, 1986) stresses the importance users attach to the worker being personal as well as professional. Some interesting consumer research by Hil (1986) and Vanstone (1986) in two different probation day centre settings (both in Pointing, 1986) demonstrated clearly that the users of the centres valued greatly the kind of informal relationship they could have with their probation officers, by contrast with what they experienced as the ritualised once-a-fortnight office interview. Thus it seems reasonable to suggest that whilst openness and a capacity to self-disclose and work with personal feelings are desirable in a field-based groupworker, they are *essential* for those working with groups and group-ings in day and residential centres. The corollary of this greater personal exposure is the potential built-in support from immediately accessible colleagues. The important topics of consultation, supervision and training for staff are covered in Chapter 7.

6 Anti-discriminatory Groupwork: Race and Gender

Most introductory groupwork texts, including previous editions of this book, pay scant attention to the influence of structural factors on group process and groupwork practice. To address this influence is to increase the complexity of the analysis of groups and the consequent approaches to practice: not to do so is both to ignore the effects of factors like class, race and gender on group experience, and to collude with the incorporation of the discriminatory and oppressive features of our society into our work with groups. As explained in the introduction to this book, a core goal of 'good practice' is to permeate all aspects of groupwork theory and practice with an anti-discriminatory perspective. Why then have a separate chapter? The reason is the early and relatively undeveloped stage we have reached in formulating this perspective in a practical form which is usable by practitioners. For a while at least most of us need to give concentrated specialist attention to these factors and their significance.

I remember – to my shame – that many years ago I used to say to some women I knew that I could not comprehend why they sometimes needed to meet in separate groups from men. If counteracting the sexist behaviour of men towards them was the main aim of the group, I continued, surely it made sense to have a mixed group with men so the latter could hear what the women experienced and work jointly on the 'problems' with them? Would that it were so simple! It took me a while to realise that there were many issues that could only be tackled properly in the absence of men because they/we are the problem, and also because in mixed groups men's presence and behaviour almost inevitably precludes the very conditions necessary for women to share their deeper experiences as women, in general and more particularly at the hands – often literally – of men. In mixed groups it is not just that men often inhibit the free expression of feelings by women, but also, particularly when women are in a minority, a dynamic often develops in which women find themselves providing a 'service' for the men. This may take the form of helping them to express their feelings, listening to their views, or modelling more open communication. The effect is to 'accommodate' the men's needs, and in the process to neglect their own.

If I am honest there is still a part of me that would like to take part in a women's or black people's group even though I am by definition not eligible! I am not sure whether this feeling is just my personal curiosity and/or whether it is primarily a gender/racial factor stemming from my need as a white male to be having some controlling influence over women and black people. I hope it is the former, but have to accept that it may well have elements of the latter. I should also mention that the most uncomfortable and unpleasant group I have ever been in was an all-male group with the here-and-now task of experiencing and understanding what was happening and what we did to each other and to ourselves as men. The purpose of these self-disclosures is to acknowledge and emphasise that we all approach these issues from the perspective of our own particular identity and life experience. This places obvious limitations on the credentials and credibility of myself, as a white middle-class male, for writing this chapter. One step I have taken to try and counteract this bias is to ask both black and white female colleagues, from agency and college settings, to read this chapter in draft and offer comments which I have subsequently tried to incorporate. Their valuable assistance is acknowledged at the beginning of the book, but this does not of course in itself legitimise what follows, which is entirely my own responsibility.

The aim of the chapter is to indicate the significance of race and gender in groupwork and how this may be taken into account in groupwork practice. The consideration of race and gender is set in the wider conceptual context of the social discrimination and oppression of many categories of people in our society and how this affects group process and the task of the groupworker. I have selected out gender and race for more detailed consideration, partly because they are of central concern to groupworkers, but also because they are two areas about which I feel relatively more able to write than, say, social class or physical disability. This is not to suggest a 'hierarchy of oppressions' (a destructive concept), rather to examine general principles in the context of particular examples. I try to indicate the transferability of some of the concepts and practice principles, and in the final section suggest a simple framework for developing an approach to practice which creates the conditions for empowerment of users whatever their source of disempowerment may be.

The term 'black' is used frequently in this chapter, and elsewhere in the book, to refer to people in Britain who because the colour of their skin is 'non-white' often experience racial discrimination: personally, culturally and institutionally. This is their common experience of racism, whether in small groups or other contexts in the wider society. However, this umbrella term includes people from many different cultures, languages and religions, as well as people who are of mixed parentage and/or bi-cultural in origin. It is therefore very important, when making generalisations of the kind that follow, also to recognise the significance of inter-ethnic differences and the uniqueness of the experience each individual brings to a group.

Three aspects of anti-discriminatory groupwork

1. Groups as a social microcosm

The evidence from research suggests that small groups are a mini version of the wider society. We all have some evidence of this from our own experience. One example occurred in a group for recently bereaved people with a predominantly working-class membership but which included a woman doctor. The rest of the group deferred to her initially as if she would somehow be more competent or able to cope than the others, when in fact her grief and emotional needs were just as great as those of anyone else. This differentiation by status was equally unhelpful for her and for the other group members. Another common example is when a white man and a black woman co-work with a group. The initial assumption, at least by the members if not also the workers, and based on how things are generally in the wider society, is usually that the white man is the 'senior' co-worker and the black woman the 'junior' partner (Mistry and Brown, 1991). Similarly in natural groups and groupings in the social context, men tend to take dominant roles *vis-à-vis* women, depending of course on the situation and the people involved.

This reproduction of 'external' social attitudes within the boundary of the group is not really surprising, and indeed what possible reason could there be for expecting it to be otherwise? There is nothing intrinsically special or different about people just because they meet together in a group! The problem is that many groupworkers behave as if all members start equal, and if they have looked at some of the standard groupwork textbooks they are unlikely to have found anything to suggest otherwise. In varying degrees texts recognise that much of what happens in groups is about power, the power of the worker(s) *vis-à-vis* the members and the power of each member relative to the other members. However, this is mainly considered in terms of intra-group dynamics and stages of development, and less commonly by emphasising the influence of structural factors on group life and power relations.

The significance of these social microcosm factors for both group composition and groupwork practice is far-reaching, because if they are not urgently and actively addressed and counteracted in the group, they will be perpetuated and reinforced. What this means for race and gender in group-work is discussed below.

2. Groups as a source of empowerment

Whereas we have just been discussing the issues which are likely to arise in groups organised for a whole range of purposes not primarily concerned with social oppression, but which will reflect discrimination unless active steps are taken, increasingly groups are being established with the primary aim of empowerment. This is a deliberate use of a group to create conditions in which members are able to regain self-esteem and more control over their own lives. Many of these groups draw on group strength and cohesion to take collective action to try and change environmental conditions whether by reducing oppressive policies and structures, obtaining additional resources, or other means.

Some groups, often therapeutically oriented (Yalom, 1975), concentrate on the strengthening of individuals. Others, mostly in the community work tradition, but some from a social groupwork base (e.g. Mullender and Ward, 1991), put the main emphasis on collective action to achieve environmental change external to the group. A third approach attempts to combine direct individual empowerment with collective external action to achieve social change (which in turn is empowering both for those who engage in it and those who benefit from it). Margot Breton's approach is an example of the latter which can be characterised as combining 'the personal and the political' in the same group's work and aims. She illustrates this by analysing the core concept of mutual aid in groupwork. She argues that it is not sufficient to restrict mutual aid in a group to what she calls the 'healing' power for individual members, but that there is a second kind of mutual aid which she calls 'liberating' power and which is harnessed collectively by group members in the pursuit of social goals (Breton, 1989). Some would say that the personal not only should not, but cannot, be separated from the political, because the development of personal growth, confidence, assertiveness and power will have the inevitable outcome of 'political' acts which challenge discriminatory social systems.

One example of the latter approach is reported and conceptualised in a recent article by Judith Lee (1991). The group was for homeless black women, who were alone or with their children. They lived in hostels in conditions of severe poverty and often had experienced violence and abuse from male partners or associates. The combined effects of these adversities, exacerbated by racism and sexism, produced personal pain, hurt and anger which the process of mutual aid in the group could go some way towards healing. However, the root of the problem lay in the combined structural oppressions of poverty, racism and sexism, so the second goal of the group was to take collective political action, for example lobbying an African-American woman mayor and organising a local protest march against homelessness. Lee conceptualises the mutual healing process as the 'pre-empowerment stage', and the social action as the 'empowerment stage', an issue I return to at the end of this chapter.

A second example of the personal/political duality is taken from a group for black students on a social work training course. This group combines the dual aims of firstly providing a support structure for individuals faced with the pain, anger and deskilling effects of racism on the course and elsewhere; and secondly mobilising group pressure for changes in the structures, curriculum and policies of the course, both in the university and the social work agencies.

I have described this dual approach in more detail than the others because it is more complex and also it embodies my personal view that empowerment comes from a combination of individual and structural change.

3. Groups for those who oppress and disempower others

A third type of group is concerned with consciousness-raising and training in anti-oppressive behaviour for people who, whether consciously or unconsciously, and whether at the personal or institutional level, contribute to the processes of disempowerment of others. Examples of these groups, often run on a workshop basis over two or three days, include disability equality groups for people without disabilities; men's groups on anti-sexism and overcoming violence; anti-racism or racial equality groups for white people; and anti-ageism groups for younger people.

These groups are by definition often tense and difficult. This is because group members are being confronted in one way or another by their own prejudices and oppressive tendencies, as well as by increased understanding of the ways in which institutions frequently do not offer genuine equal opportunities, thus favouring people in their position compared to those from the oppressed group. A further aspect is that increased power for previously disempowered groups often means reduced power and control for those who have benefited from the hitherto unequal power distribution. For example, if 50 per cent of the directors of Social Services Departments in Britain were to be women, instead of the present 10 per cent or so, fewer men than at present would have the opportunity to become directors. This is a very obvious and simple example but it illustrates the point. Anti-oppressive groups often elicit guilt and anxiety in their participants, but if the groups are to achieve their aims they need, *inter alia*, to contribute to changed behaviour by individuals and to acceptance of a redistribution of power in organisations and other systems.

Another positive aspect of these kinds of groups, and one not often emphasised, is the potential for the 'oppressor' to be empowered in the sense of becoming liberated from being a stereotype of his kind towards being more a whole person. An example of this process occurred in a fathers' group established at a family centre for the partners of women attending a neighbourhood group. The focus was on how to become better fathers through more involvement in child care, and more supportive partners through a more involved sharing relationship. Thus by letting go of the oppressive and constraining power associated with a traditional 'macho' male role, some of these men were liberated to enjoy a much wider range and quality of experiences (personal communication, Mistry, 1991).

A gender perspective on groupwork

Women meeting together on their own in groups has been a central feature of the development of feminism and the study of women's issues in the last 30 years. The group medium has proved to be a very effective way of supporting individual women facing the struggles of living in a male-dominated society; of creating a collective base for action for equality and justice for women, particularly in the sphere of social policy; and for the articulation of feminist theory, gender studies and research. All these developments in the 1960s and 1970s occurred mostly outside social work, although many women social workers participated as individuals. In a book on groupwork it is interesting and important to note the significance that people meeting in groups can have for activity and impact which has potential far beyond what a group offers to the individual member.

This development has had a profound effect on groupwork in the social work context in the last decade. Many women social workers (and the occasional man!) have introduced feminist perspectives into their overall approach to practice and to groupwork in particular. They have identified the need for women, whether they be users or staff, to meet on their own in groups for some purposes. These moves often encounter resistance from male staff (and male partners/relatives) essentially because women meeting in groups provide a source of strength through shared experiences, and a potential increase in control over their own lives, whether as members of the community or the agency, and this is a threat to male dominance.

Examples of these trends can be found in the recent groupwork literature. Donnelly (1986) describes the development of a self-help group linked to a voluntary agency. Some women staff formed an alliance with women living on a large city estate characterised by poverty, social disadvantage and despair. A community-oriented feminist approach based on a partnership between workers and users focused on the issues of power, gender and poverty which faced the women on the estate. The group was able both to address the individual needs of the women and collectively to undertake social campaigning to improve community living conditions. There is no doubt that the women were empowered by this approach and experienced not only real hope but actual achievement.

In the statutory setting of the probation service Mistry (1989) and her female co-workers successfully established a women offenders' group where previously there had been no suitable provision for women, who typically were a marginalised minority expected to fit in with a male-dominated groupwork ethos. This group spawned its own second stage self-help group for women after they completed their statutory obligations. Two years later this 'move-on' group had been discontinued due to lack of resources, a timely reminder that sustaining developments of this kind is a constant difficulty. Influenced by Mistry's account and by feminist writings on women and the criminal justice system, similar developments of specialist groups for female offenders have occurred in other probation areas. One example of such a group has been recorded by M. Jones *et al.* (1991), whose account emphasises that not only were the offenders themselves empowered by the groupwork experience, but so were the women staff, to the extent that they were able to influence agency policy on services for women offenders. A significant factor in this development was the committed involvement of a female line-manager and both male and female support at senior management level.

The above examples are illustrative of some of the ways in which women-centred groupwork has been a major influence on the general development of groupwork. In addition to the creation of an approach which views the personal and the political as inextricably linked, women's groups have also had an influence on the *methods* used. A good example of this is seen in the book by Ernst and Goodison (1982) which, in the process of articulating guide-lines for running self-help groups for personal growth and awareness for women, describes many group games and activities which are equally suitable for men's groups and mixed groups. Ernst and others at the Women's Therapy Centre in London have produced several collections of papers (see Ernst and Maguire, 1987; Krzowski and Land, 1988), further outlining different kinds of women's groups. A new book specifically on feminist groupwork has just been published at the time of writing (Butler and Wintram, 1991).

So far I have concentrated on the female gender, but another important consequence of the development of women's groups is the growing interest in recent years in groups for men. Some of these have broad agendas concerned with a whole range of men's issues and consciousness-raising, and many focus specifically on male violence and other oppressive behaviours. An example of the former are awareness groups (see for example McLeod and Pemberton, 1987), and of the latter are groups for male perpetrators of sexual abuse (see for example Cowburn, 1990). McLeod and Pemberton make interesting comments about the ways in which all-male therapy groups require men to develop various skills and attributes, such as self-disclosure, intimacy and open expression of feeling, which in mixed groups they tend to leave to women members. They also observe that in an all-male group men can learn to separate out sexual expression from intimacy, and then use this ability in relationships with women where previously the men had equated closeness with sexuality.

The literature on men's groups is quite sparse, particularly on those numerous groups, unlike the two cited above, whose primary task is not concerned with gender or gender-related behaviour. For instance we know very little about the extent to which male workers or co-workers give any priority to the importance of working to develop an anti-sexist culture with members in their all-male groups.

To the British-based references should be added those cited above from North America (Breton, 1989; and Lee, 1991). Also Garvin and Reed (1983) have co-edited a very useful double issue of *Social Work with Groups* on gender issues, which includes a range of important articles on both men's and women's groups. Much of the research on gender (and class and race) and small groups is usefully summarised and referenced in Davis and Proctor (1989).

A race perspective on groupwork

Whilst race and ethnicity have begun to feature more prominently on the groupwork agenda in recent years on both sides of the Atlantic, much less has been published and conceptualised than on gender. This makes it difficult to identify and articulate a clear race perspective at this stage of development of practice and theory. There are of course some similarities stemming from the common experience that black people and women have of social oppression, but there are also important differences.

The first is the different historical explanation of the origins of gender and race oppression. Whereas the former is to be found predominantly in the family, the latter derives from white imperialism and its post-colonial manifestation in contemporary Western European countries.

The second is the obvious numerical difference. Whereas women have numerical equality with men in the wider society, black people make up only 5 per cent of the British population, though of course with wide variations in different parts of the country. This means that black people constantly find themselves to be the only black person in an otherwise white group. This creates all kinds of pressures on that person making it extremely unlikely that, if indeed they stay in the group, they will benefit to the extent that they would in either a more evenly mixed group or an all-black group. On the other hand women can generally expect to find themselves with at least numerically equal representation in mixed groups, if not equal power. There are however important exceptions to this where women find themselves in a small minority. These are not only in the halls of power (for example senior politicians, managers, judges, professors and industrialists) but in certain user groups such as offenders, mentioned earlier.

Thirdly, due not least to institutional racism in education, there are few black academic writers and researchers on groupwork, whereas women have for many years had a wide representation and prominence in social work education, enabling them to try and ensure that a gender perspective influences social groupwork theory and practice.

Fourthly, black women face the 'double jeopardy' in groups and elsewhere of being both female and black, and there is a black critique (see for example Shah's 'It's up to you sisters: black women and radical social work' in Langan and Lee, 1989) of those white feminist perspectives which ignore the experience of black women.

One consequence of the marginalisation of black perspectives in groupwork theory and practice development has been, at least in Britain, an almost entirely ethnocentric approach to groupwork. This approach is seen in the type of groupwork models created, whether out of ethnocentric practice experience or ethnocentric academic thinking. The consequences are seen in the assumptions about what is 'good groupwork', the conventions, the methods, the philosophy and so on. Black social work students have said to me, with some justification, that the groupwork I teach and write about is 'white' groupwork. They could also have added 'and middle-class'. I believe that whilst I and others like me have a responsibility to respond to this issue as best we can in all our groupwork involvement, the turning point will come as black groupworkers and academics develop a groupwork which is responsive to the needs of black members and those of different ethnicities. This process has already started (see literature references below).

Turning to developments in practice, the last decade has seen the growth of black groups both inside and outside social work, and in particular among community groups in the voluntary sector. Most of these groups have the dual function identified in women's groups of providing both personal support for individuals facing the oppression of racism, and a forum for acting collectively to combat institutional discrimination. The establishment of black student groups on social work training courses referred to earlier is a good example. These groups were created out of the desperate need of black students, who typically found themselves in a small minority on their course and experiencing all the additional pressures arising from high visibility and covert – and sometimes overt – racism both in the college and on practice placements. These groups can offer both a safe place for individual sharing, and a forum for identifying action for change in the course environment, curriculum, policies and other areas in which discrimination is experienced. Examples among user groups include groups for older Asian people in day centres, and a Centre in Handsworth for Afro-Caribbeans (Green, 1987).

Davis and Proctor (1989) have summarised the available research information about the race dimension in groupwork. Their findings have to be qualified in two ways. Firstly, as with much social psychological research, the participants were frequently drawn from the American student population, whose behaviour is not necessarily similar to, say, that of working-class youth in disadvantaged inner city areas in Britain! Secondly, as pointed out by Ward (1990), their study does not address the impact of the macro dimension of institutional discrimination. Bearing in mind these important caveats, the following points emerge from their survey of the literature:

1. Individuals are most comfortable with those who are racially similar.
2. Neither white nor black members like to be racially outnumbered (although elsewhere Davis has drawn attention to the important concept of the 'psychological majority'. This is used to describe the phenomenon when black members are not in a numerical majority but are 'over-represented' proportionately compared to the general population, Davis, 1980).
3. Racially heterogeneous groups may be more complex and difficult to facilitate.
4. Group leaders do not vary their behaviour according to

racial composition but members behave differently according to the race of the leader. Same-race leaders are generally viewed more positively.

5.   Very little is known about bi-racial co-leadership (but see Mistry and Brown, 1991).

6.   Some ethnic minority members, for example Latinos (Werbin and Hines, 1975) prefer an active informal leadership style because traditionally they rely on informal support systems. *Note*: It is, however, dangerous to generalise as there can be wide variations between minority ethnic groups. Hong Kong Chinese people, for example, expect structure and a degree of formality (Pearson, 1991).

7.   Both black and white members provide same-race members with more honest feedback.

8.   Black members who perform less competently in groups get a less positive response than do their white counterparts in similar circumstances.

9.   There are important variations among members from different ethnic minorities, for example on readiness to self-disclose and in politeness/confrontation.

10.   There is no clear evidence about the effect of racial group composition on outcome, and similarly with the race of the worker, except that for the latter, previous experience of working with people from ethnic minorities is an advantage.

11.   Group approaches which are culturally sensitive, concrete, actively led and environmentally focused and give immediate attention to problem-resolution are in general viewed positively by ethnic minority participants.

Davis and Proctor go on to suggest 'guidelines for practice' (pp. 118–23) and some of these are subsumed in the practice guidelines below.

Another interesting piece of research was undertaken by Brower *et al.* (in Lassner *et al.*, eds, 1987) into 'Exploring the Effects of Leader Gender and Race on Group Behaviour'. Variations in group members' behaviour and attitudes according to the race and gender of the groupworker were studied. There is only space here to summarise the overall finding that '. . . gender and ethnicity . . . have an impact on group situations that may be of equal force to the variables we customarily seek to affect such as program, leadership technique, group composition and so forth.' This provides further evidence of the centrality of race and gender in social groupwork.

An examination of published practice and theory-building accounts suggests that in the USA particular attention is given to ethnicity and multi-cultural aspects (e.g. Comaz-Diaz, 1984 on Puerto Rican women; J. Brown, 1984 on low-income black youths; Freeman and McRoy, 1986 on un-employed black teenagers; Edwards and Edwards, 1984 on American Indians; Delgado and Humm-Delgado, 1984 on Hispanics), contrasting with a British emphasis on racism (Muston and Weinstein, 1988; Rhule, 1988; Mullender, 1988). An edited UK book on *Groupwork in Adoption and Foster Care* (Triseliotis, 1988) has three chapters which address race and cultural factors in fostering and adoption.

A leading contributor to practice-theory on 'ethnicity and biculturalism' in the USA is Chau (1990a and 1990b). Building on the special issue of *Social Work with Groups* on 'ethnicity in social groupwork practice' (Davis, 1984), Chau (1990a) points out that in an increasingly multi-racial society there is an urgent need for 'culturally competent practice'. This means addressing cultural factors in every aspect of groupwork planning and practice. He goes on to say that in order to be able to do this social work trainers must revise the traditional groupwork syllabus.

The British emphasis on anti-racism and the need for a black perspective in social groupwork is highlighted in an article by a black woman (Rhule 1988) who co-led with a white colleague a group for white women with black children, the aim being to address the needs of the black children growing up in a white environment. She describes very vividly the pressures on her as the only black person in a group permeated by white racism, and how despite the support and encouragement of her white colleague, she experienced a basic need to obtain consultancy for herself from a black consultant. She also questions the acceptability of placing a black person in that position of isolation, pain and pressure. This account of her experience raises a number of practice issues which are incorporated in the practice guidelines which now follow.

Practice guidelines for an anti-discriminatory approach to race and gender in groupwork

Whilst these guidelines refer particularly to race and gender, many of them can be treated as a general anti-discriminatory approach to groupwork, with suitable adaptation being made for ageism, disablism, heterosexism and so on. It is important that the necessary simplification to consider particular variables or forms of oppression does not result in a 'single issue' approach. For example, black males and heterosexual females may be in positions where they are 'oppressor' in respect of one form of discrimination and 'oppressed' in relation to another.

1. General

Race and gender should be central to all aspects of groupwork research, theory, policy and practice. This means that for the practitioner questions about race and gender should be just as routine as 'where will the group meet?' or 'what will the programme be?' Agency policies on groupwork need to consider what 'equal opportunities' will actually involve structurally and in resource terms if equal access to appropriate group services is to become a reality for women and people from minority ethnic groups. Policy-makers will need to be open to 'bottom-up' influences by setting up lines of communication in which the views of female, black and other staff, and actual and potential users of groupwork services, can be expressed and taken seriously.

Creating equal opportunities in groupwork services for oppressed groups in the population is a more obvious form of anti-discriminatory groupwork than working anti-oppressively with groups which are composed entirely of those who are part of an identified oppression. Groups for white people that are specifically about racism and groups for men that are specifically about sexism will by definition address these issues. However, there are many all-male groups (with male workers) whose primary task is something quite different, for example probation groups to confront offending behaviour, where unless strenuous efforts are made by aware male workers there is likely to be a group culture of sexist collusion. Similarly in all-white groups (with white workers), for example a parents' group in a family centre, an ethnocentric if not overtly racist culture is likely to develop unless the white workers consciously and deliberately address race issues proactively. In both these examples one possible way of reducing the often unconscious collusive approach is to make arrangements for a consultant from the relevant oppressed population.

2. Planning stage

(a) Group composition (see also Chapter 2). The first question is whether the group should be mixed or separate according to gender and/or race. There will be 'in principle' criteria, for example separate provision being desirable when issues of racial or gender identity and experience are likely to be central to group purpose; and practical criteria, for example will a woman be significantly less likely to benefit from a particular group if it includes men, and will having a mixed-race group mean that there will be only one or two black members, who will almost certainly be disadvantaged as a result? The corollary of this is that if a mixed group is planned, strenuous efforts need to be made to seek a group composition which is not too skewed in its membership and liable to marginalisation of some members. 'Parents' groups' are a good example: frequently these are offered without any clear indication whether there is a serious intention to include fathers as well as mothers, one or two fathers turn up at the beginning and then drift away.

The second question concerns the choice of the co-workers, or identity of the single worker. As a generalisation, if a group is composed of all the same sex or all the same race, there need to be good reasons for not having a worker or co-workers of the same sex/race. The anti-collusion arguments for having, say, a female worker in an otherwise all-male group (Weaver and Fox, 1984), or a black worker in an otherwise all-white group (Rhule, 1988), are likely to be stronger than the 'positive role-model' arguments used for having a male worker in an otherwise all-female group or a white worker in an otherwise all-black group. A central issue in the former situation is likely to be the degree of pressure and stereotyping put on the worker, and in the latter case the potentially inhibiting and distracting effects on the group members. In Masson and Erooga's discussion (1990) of male/female co-worker composition in a group for mothers of sexually abused children, they acknowledge that the presence of a man had some inhibiting effects on the women, but say there were important compensatory advantages deriving from a 'positive model of maleness'.

If membership is mixed it may be desirable to have that mix reflected in the gender/race balance of the co-workers, and in particular to have at least one co-worker with whom the discriminated-against members can identify: this means at least one female worker in a mixed-gender group, and at least one black co-worker in a mixed-race group. Mistry and Brown (1991) discuss black/white co-working issues in general, including the not infrequent situation where the ethnicity of the black co-worker may be different from that of some or all of the black members.

The above discussion has assumed that there can be some control over the composition of a group. There are of course many instances in practice when this is not possible and a group ends up with a membership which is almost certainly disadvantaging to some minority members, but the only alternative to which may be no provision at all. One way round this difficulty, which is now being tried in some agencies, is to make group provision across a wider catchment area – say that of several social work teams or even a whole city in urban areas (see Mackintosh, 1991) – so that groups can be composed in ways which counteract the marginalisation of particular categories of service users. In the short term it is not always possible to address these structural and organisational problems, and the minority user should if possible be offered the choice about whether to continue in the group. If she decides to continue it is then the responsibility of the worker(s) to take steps in the group to minimise her disadvantage, and outside the group to ensure that appropriate support structures are available if needed.

(b) Supervision/consultation.   Consideration of race and gender in choice of supervisor or consultant is crucially affected by the reality that whilst consultants are chosen, supervisors are given! One of the arguments for having a consultant as well as, or instead of, a supervisor may well be

that the gender/racial identity of the supervisor is not appropriate for some of the assistance which one or both co-workers are seeking. The woman worker in a male-dominated group or the black worker in a white-dominated group will almost inevitably face additional pressures due to the respective sexism and racism in the group behaviour and culture. This is both hurtful and exhausting whether working alone or with a partner of the same gender/race as the dominant group, however sympathetic and supportive the latter may be. In these circumstances it is essential to have access to a supervisor/consultant who shares the same identity and perspective. For a black worker with a white co-worker and all-white group, or a female worker with a male co-worker and an all-male group, the choice should be available of having appropriate one-to-one consultancy *in addition to* whatever arrangements are made for joint consultancy for the co-workers as a pair (Rhule, 1988). Another important role for a consultant is in those situations where the worker(s), however unwittingly, have got into a collusive discriminatory alliance with the group members. In these circumstances the consultant's heightened awareness of anti-discrimination issues, whether due to their own experience of oppression and/or their well developed level of awareness, can play a vital role in challenging the workers and pointing out things that they may have missed through being part of the group dynamic.

This discussion has concentrated on the choice of consult-ant with an implicit suggestion that consultancy per se is desirable. It was stated earlier that it is very difficult for co-workers to sort out difficulties in their own co-working relationship without the assistance of a third person. This is even more difficult when complex and strongly felt issues of race and gender are prominent in the group and in the concerns of the co-workers. It also means that consultancy is needed from someone who not only has the appropriate identity but who has the necessary competence based on a personally worked out understanding of race and gender discrimination and the strong feelings that are aroused.

(c) Style, format, culture of group.   It seems (see Thomas, 1986) that many black people either do not join a group in the first place or they may leave it prematurely because,

often quite unconsciously, the (probably) white organisers have not taken cultural diversity or racism into account in their programme ideas and general approach. For example a parenting group for a multi-racial membership needs to be responsive to cultural differences in child-rearing patterns including the central role of the extended family in some cultures, and the clear role-differences between male and female parents in others: and a social skills group preparing members for job interviews needs to recognise that black interviewees have to face racial discrimination as well as all the other general problems when seeking employment. The location of the group may be very important for ethnic minority users, who are likely to be more convinced that the group may have something to offer them if it is located in a neighbourhood in which many of them live. Similarly the visual images presented in the group room and the actual materials and resources available can be either user-friendly for black members or alienating. I am not advocating window-dressing of a superficial kind: if the images are not consistent with the group experience and the perspectives of the workers in how they actually behave and respond in the group then this is worse than a group which is unambiguously ethnocentric throughout: the latter at least enables the potential black member to make an informed choice not to join the group in the first place.

3. Same race/same gender groups

The first issue is establishing the need for race-specific or gender-specific groups using the criteria and points mentioned earlier in this chapter. Such moves often encounter resistance, particularly from the 'excluded' race/gender staff who sometimes seek to strengthen their case by producing supporters from the 'included' gender/race. Examples of this resistance and ways of overcoming it have been documented: Muston and Weinstein (1988) give an example of the quite irrational and obviously racist opposition from white social workers to supporting the formation by a black worker of a group for black older people on a housing estate. First they declared that there were hardly any black elders on the estate, then that there was no need for a group anyway, then when both these points were disproven that there were no good reasons for not having a mixed-membership group! The fact that numerous white-only groups had been run for decades without question was not apparently seen as relevant! Two recent articles on the formation of women's groups in the probation service (Mistry, 1989; Jones *et al.*, 1991) refer to the initial resistance from male colleagues and managers to accepting the need for separate provision. This phenomenon is sometimes mirrored by users, for example by the not infrequent reactions of male partners who resent and resist their female partner participating in a women's group which raises her consciousness and helps her to be more assertive.

The second point is obtaining legitimacy from the agency that this type of group is not a fringe activity to be tolerated but a core provision for particular groups of users. Creating the conditions for this recognition often needs an alliance of several workers with one or more senior managers who are sympathetic, and also requires political skills and determination. In practice what usually happens is that the first such groups have to be run as a marginal activity on inadequate resources to demonstrate their value and effectiveness as a precondition of acceptance. Once they are accepted the problem is how to sustain the necessary positive conditions for running the groups. Relying on one or two sympathetic senior managers is not sufficient in the longer term because these key people may leave and be replaced by others who take a different view. It is therefore important to try and get the necessary change in the agency to secure the kind of infrastructure which is a prerequisite for anti-discriminatory group provision.

The third consideration is adequate resourcing, both in staffing and funding. This in turn may involve organisational flexibility. For example, it may mean that in order to provide a group for Asian children with learning difficulties it is necessary to pool resources across several social work teams and to spend more funds on transporting group members from a wider catchment area. It may also mean paying for consultation from a suitably qualified Asian groupwork consultant if no such person is available in the agency.

A fourth point is that almost by definition these groups will develop social action agendas as consciousness is raised, and this is likely to be experienced as threatening by established interests in the agency and quite possibly also in the community. Workers, particularly in statutory agencies, may face quite acute conflicts of loyalty between their identification with their agency as their employer and their identification with the group members as people who face precisely the same kind of oppression as themselves. This issue needs to be anticipated and prepared for preferably with the assistance of a consultant who understands the issues involved.

4. 'Mixed' groups

We will now discuss guidelines for working with groups that are mixed by gender and/or race, bearing in mind that they may be mixed either by choice or necessity and this is likely to affect the dynamics and the approach taken.

(a) Putting race and gender on the agenda.   A core skill for groupworkers is an ability to put race and gender (and other forms of discrimination) 'on the agenda' from the beginning of the first meeting of the group and to keep them there until the end – not just as a group topic but as a core dimension of all that the group does. The purpose of this is to legitimise these issues as important ones which group members are encouraged to raise as and when they wish. For the inexperienced worker who is still clarifying their own position and awareness of discrimination this may have to be done in a rather conscious and deliberate way at first. The position to aim for is one in which an anti-discriminatory perspective and approach becomes so much a part of you that your every behaviour immediately conveys to group members, and particularly those from oppressed minorities, an understanding that this issue will not only be taken seriously but will be central to the work of the group.

Part of this core skill is to avoid a 'single-issue' approach to anti-discrimination. It is hard to think of any group in which, whilst one particular oppression may be the most obvious and pressing, several others are not potentially important issues for the group. This approach can also be empowering for group members who can get trapped into being labelled as spokespersons only for their own overt oppression. In an article on preparing social work students for anti-discriminatory practice on placement, Margaret Boushel (1991) discusses this issue and gives an example of a black woman student who included in her feedback on the workshop the following comment: 'I feel really strongly about disability and it was good to be able to say that. Some white students think that because you're black race is the only issue you care about.'

(b) Groundrules. Virtually all groups need some ground-rules which will govern how members – and workers – behave and treat each other in the group. Examples of these might be that everyone in the group will have an equal opportunity to contribute and participate, that everyone will be respected for what and who they are, that there will be no violence and that sexist and racist and other discriminatory language or behaviour is unacceptable. Any groundrules which may be laid down by the agency or setting will automatically apply to the group, others will be group-specific. Some will be stated by the workers, others will be negotiable. Workers need to be very clear who will determine the groundrules for any particular group, and what is and what is not negotiable. When groundrules are already determined by the setting, for example a groundrule prohibiting any form of violence in an Intermediate Treatment centre including the violence of racist behaviour (see Ball and Sowa, 1989), this can be a big advantage.

Establishing a groundrule does not of course mean that it will necessarily be adhered to, but it does mean that if it is breached both workers and members have a mandate for confronting the transgressing behaviour. In practice it is often only when such an incident occurs and is confronted that the groundrule takes on real meaning and significance in the experience of the members.

(c) A proactive approach. As stated earlier, groups will inevitably reproduce social patterns of discrimination unless active steps are taken to counteract these processes. Firstly this requires the groupworkers to be vigilant about their own group behaviour and to make sure that they model the inclusion and involvement of all the members on an equal basis. This is easier said than done, and one trap is to overcompensate by, for example, overprotecting black

members in a kind of inverted racism. Secondly, it requires the groupworker to take action when a group member is being treated unequally by other group members. This may be because of their sex, status, age, disability or the colour of their skin. As outlined in Chapter 4 there are both indirect and direct ways of doing this: indirect methods include behaviours which validate the marginalised member and restrain oppression-related dominance, for example by men in the group; and direct methods which make explicit in the group what is happening and invite group members to examine group process and discuss how to re-establish genuine equality of opportunity and treatment. In order to do this the worker needs to have a clearly worked out personal position on the issues. Thirdly, the worker needs to be active outside the group, for example in ensuring that the environment of the group is one which proclaims the anti-discriminatory ethos rather than contradicts it. Black women in a mothers' group in a family centre in a multi-racial area may not be impressed by the white worker's apparent commitment to an anti-discriminatory approach if there are no black images in the children's room and no attempts are being made to recruit black staff to the centre.

(d) Cultural and identity considerations. In this chapter all people from non-white minority ethnic groups have been referred to as 'black'. This omits very important cultural differences that may be represented in a group, by for example people of Jamaican, Pakistani, Iranian and Irish origins. There is of course the prior question about whether there is a justification for including such a range of diversity in the same group. When a group is multi-cultural in composition it is essential that the programme and style of the group recognises, validates and reflects ethnic differences and customs. In order to do this the worker needs to have at least some basic understanding of the customs and cultures of group members. An important skill is responding to incidents or interactions which indicate prejudice and ignorance among group members about each other's customs and beliefs.

There are also increasing numbers of people in Britain who are of 'mixed parentage', a term that is used to describe those of bi-cultural or multi-ethnic origin. The political division of people into 'black' and 'white', necessary as that is when considering racism, discrimination and racial inequality, is an over-simplified paradigm for considering the position of those of mixed parentage. It is therefore important that groupworkers are sensitive to the position and feelings of group members in this position, and that however racism and associated issues are being approached in the group due attention and space is given to those group members who do not fit neatly into other people's definitions.

(e) Confronting racism, sexism amd other forms of discrimination when they occur in the group or in the setting of the group. This requires of the worker a capacity to intervene and confront unacceptable behaviour in a way which challenges the behaviour without condemning the perpetrator of it – not an easy task. In my experience white people and men tend to get involved in long debates about when and when not to respond, whereas for many black people and women there is no question of not intervening when they encounter racism or sexism respectively, just of how to do it and how to cope with the strong feelings and anger that may be evoked. Ideally one would hope that the group members themselves would reach a point when they would take on much of the responsibility for making the challenges and establishing a group culture and spirit in which oppressive behaviour becomes increasingly unlikely. As was made clear earlier, this last point applies as much to groups for 'oppressors' whose primary task is not directly concerned with oppression, as it does to groups in which the recipients of discrimination are present and those whose primary task is to do with discrimination.

(f) Establishing trust. This takes time in almost any group, and is likely to take longer and more effort in multiracial and mixed-gender groups. Other things being equal, women are more likely to trust other women than men, and similarly black people are more likely to trust other black people than whites. This applies to both inter-member and member–worker attitudes and relationships. Workers and members often do not know what other members' past experiences have been, yet these are likely to have a

profound effect on their capacity to trust other people in the group. This is precisely why it is often preferable to have race-specific and gender-specific groups when deeper, more personal matters are likely to be on the agenda.

(g) Programme content, method and style.   In the more structured kinds of groups which use significant preplanned content, as for example in some social skills groups, and group 'packages', great care needs to be taken to ensure that the content, method and style are appropriate to the particular membership of the group. All exercises, questionnaires, games, role-plays and other devices need to be checked for gender bias, ethnocentrism, heterosexism, ageism, class bias, disablism and so on. For someone who faces bias and marginalisation daily in their lives it is likely to be a matter of great importance whether the group simply reproduces their experience or whether it gives a refreshing indication that their identity and interests have been regarded as central to the group orientation and programme. We cannot and will not always get it right first time, and openness to critical feedback is an essential basis for constantly improving the quality and appropriateness of group content. In groups where the members have the major say in programme content and topics, the worker has a responsibility to try and ensure that these guidelines are observed and that individual members are not marginalised in the group process. This is quite delicate and poses certain interventionist dilemmas for the worker, which will be considerably reduced if the group has established guidelines as part of a contract which binds members and workers to an anti-discriminatory approach.

(h) External support systems.   As noted earlier, group-workers will frequently find themselves working with groups in far from ideal conditions, as for example in day or residential settings where they may have little or no control over group composition or other key factors. In these circumstances a prior decision is whether to refuse to participate unless certain minimal conditions are met. This may be easier said than done particularly if participation is a management requirement and/or it would disadvantage group users not to take part. In these circumstances the

worker needs to take steps to try and compensate for the disadvantage. For example if there are only one or two black members available for a group, and they are keen to participate albeit as a small minority, the worker may be able to help these members to be linked also to some appropriate black group which can provide a source of support and strength. Another possibility is that some additional one-to-one contact, preferably with a black member of staff, is provided as back-up outside the group.

5. Co-working issues

These have been considered in some detail in Chapter 3, both in general and the specific issues arising with black/white and male/female co-working. Suffice it here to repeat that the racial and gender composition of the co-working pair *will* affect both the members' perceptions and behaviour in the group, and the workers' feelings and behaviour in their working relationship. The form this will take will of course vary according to the type of group, the clientele, the workers and the context. The important thing is to ensure that the co-workers include in their preparation an open and honest sharing of their own feelings, attitudes and expectations about both their co-working relationship and what may happen for each of them as individuals in the group. The crucial role of consultancy in facilitating this process has already been emphasised.

A framework for empowerment in groupwork

An anti-discriminatory approach to groupwork involves much more than the 'negative' achievement of confronting different forms of discrimination in and around the group: it is an approach which seeks actively to empower the group participants and particularly those who have been disempowered in the wider society because of their class, colour, sex, disability, age, religion or sexual orientation. 'Empowerment' has become a fashionable and easily abused concept, but that need not detract from its importance. Groupwork is a method of social work particularly well suited to creating the conditions for people to discover and realise their potential and value, both in the group and in what they can take from the group to influence their living environment and help them take more control over their own lives.

A few writers have begun the task of conceptualising the notion of empowerment in groupwork and relating it to models of practice. Mullender and Ward (1991) devote the first chapter of their explication of the *Self-Directed* model to an analysis of empowerment in groupwork. They emphasise the significance of 'oppression' and 'power' in a structural framework upon which they base the practice model developed in subsequent chapters. Reference was made earlier in this chapter to Lee's paper (1991) on 'Empowerment Through Mutual Aid Groups: A Practice Grounded Conceptual Framework'. After discussing empowerment theory (as in Solomon, 1976), Lee goes on to elucidate a two- stage process of 'pre-empowerment' in which the group members (homeless women) express their personal hurt and offer each other mutual aid, followed by 'empowerment' in which they become able to take collective social action to alleviate their appalling social conditions.

To conclude this chapter I suggest a simple framework for an empowering/anti-discriminatory approach to groupwork, noting that one person cannot empower another, but that what the worker can do is help to create the conditions in which the empowerment of others can occur. The framework has five components: worker self-preparation; agency preparation; work in the group; work with other agencies; work in the group members' environment.

(1) Worker self-preparation.   As in all forms of social work, a prerequisite for effective practice is undertaking the necessary work on self-awareness and consciousness-raising. Unless the groupworker has a reasonably well worked out position in relation to their own gender and racial identity, whether they be a member of an oppressive or an oppressed group or both, male or female, black or white, they will get into all kinds of messes when these issues arise with members in the group and/or in other arenas. Similar personal preparation is necessary in respect of class, disability, age and sexual orientation, the relative importance of each of these varying according to the type of group, its

aims and likely dynamic and themes. Some suggestions on what form this training might take are made in Chapter 7.

(2) Agency and setting preparation. In Chapter 2 we emphasised the importance of the organisational environment being facilitative if a group is to be effective. This applies particularly strongly when we are considering anti-discriminatory/empowering practice. If the agency, or at least the setting in which the group is located, has a clearly worked out anti-discriminatory policy and perspective, this will be of immeasurable assistance in creating empowering conditions for the group and its members. Conversely if the agency attitude and practice is incongruent with that of the workers their task will be extremely difficult. Just as the relevant anti-discriminatory training of the groupworkers is essential, so is the relevant preparation of senior management and the whole agency environment.

Indicators of an agency's approach include: the way the organisation meets the needs of all its employees (are they empowered or diminished?); how it actually implements declared Equal Opportunities Policies; the extent to which it takes positive action to facilitate access to services for disadvantaged groups; its staffing recruitment policy in relation to minority groups; and the degree of flexibility in employment policy, for example flexible working conditions to facilitate child care arrangements. The groupworker employee who experiences an empowering environment for herself in the organisation is much more likely to be able to help create that kind of environment for others in the group.

(3) Work in the group itself. The intra-group elements of empowerment are the most obvious ones and have been considered in detail elsewhere in this chapter and in the book as a whole.

(4) Work with other agencies involved with actual and potential group members. Workers have many opportunities to influence the practice if not the policies of other agencies. For example: the probation officer writing a social enquiry report for a criminal court on a black female offender; the hospital social worker in a clinical team with patients for whom English is a second language; the school

social worker involved with non-attending children whose families are living in abject poverty; challenging the sexist police or prison officer; and so on. There may be considerable risk-taking in these arenas where the worker does not carry formal authority, and the degree of support from her or his own agency will be a crucial factor.

(5) Work in the group environment.   I have never subscribed to group models which are antagonistic to the groupworker having any involvement or even interest in the external environment of the members. The individual group member will often not be able to take on their oppressive social environment on their own, and will need the support if not the active involvement of the group members and the workers. This means the groupworker having contacts with the relevant communities and agencies in the group members' social context. There will of course have to be limits to intervention in this limitless terrain, but to eschew all external contact is hard to reconcile with a serious concern with empowerment.

A quotation from Breton's article on groupwork practice with marginalised populations provides a challenging comment on the role of the groupworker:

> However the times are such that social workers cannot afford the luxury of looking only at what goes on inside groups. Perhaps even working at the interface of groups and communities is not quite enough. As the situations of marginalised populations become more desperate, the task of influencing social policy urgently beckons all social workers. (Breton, 1991, page 46)

7 Developing Groupwork Skills and Understanding

This chapter considers firstly the basic *training* necessary for skilled groupwork practice, and then discusses *consultation/ supervision*, *recording* and *evaluation*, all three of which are important elements in the development of group skills and understanding. The chapter concludes with a qualitative evaluation by a group member of how he benefited from membership of a particular group.

Training

Groupwork training has several ingredients:

Experiential understanding of group membership. Whatever type of groupwork a social worker expects to practise, she needs to develop sensitive understanding of group processes and the role of group member. This is done primarily through experiencing and learning about her own feelings and behaviour as a group member in interaction with others. There are several ways of doing this.

The first is through participating in here-and-now groups which have the task of studying individual and group behaviour, as it happens. Groups of this kind are often described as 'training' or sensitivity' groups, and include the T-group, Tavistock group and other models (Shaffer and Galinsky, 1974; Palmer, 1978). They vary in the emphasis placed upon power, authority, intimacy, relationships, stereotyping and the group as a system, but all include an intensive exploration of the feelings which people have about themselves and others in groups. This kind of training sensitises the practitioner to the irrational and unconscious forces which influence group behaviour and the task. The origins of these forces are a complex combination of intra-psychic, interpersonal and socially imposed factors. The first two of these are well documented in the literature, but it is only more recently that attention has been given to the ways in which groups import the social stereotyping and discrimination of the wider society (see Chapter 6). Sensitivity training is one way in which the trainee can learn how his own gender, age, 'race' and class, and that of other group members, are affecting his behaviour, attitudes and feelings in groups, and that of others towards him.

Secondly, there are existing work groups, for example the student seminar group, the social work team or the hostel staff group, which may include understanding of their own process as part of their programme. An external consultant is likely to be needed to help with this task. The advantage of pursuing this learning in a 'real' group to which you belong is the direct authenticity of that situation: the disadvantage is that you may not feel as free to disclose and risk honestly as you would in a 'stranger' sensitivity group relatively free of later repurcussions. On some groupwork training courses, groups are created with a task blending conceptual and experiential understanding of group processes. For example, at Bristol University we have developed a group learning model in which feedback on how process has affected task achievement is integral to the way of learning.

Thirdly, opportunities may occur to work on personal problems and issues as a member of a therapeutic or problem-solving group, thus gaining first hand experience of what it is like to seek help from others in a group. In some group therapies, such as group analysis, transactional analysis, psychodrama and gestalt, substantial member experience is a required part of training and qualification. A modified version of this is the Shared Decision Making model developed by Maple (1977), in which a peer training group of five or six persons has one member in turn 'presenting' a problem (professional or personal) which the others have to concentrate on helping them resolve by identifying a change goal and possible methods of approaching it.

A fourth approach uses games and simulation exercises. The most effective ones are those where the trainee is asked to participate in the exercise as authentically as possible as herself, as distinct from role-playing. In one sense the less script the better because then whatever the trainee does comes from them and says something important about how they behave in unstructured group situations.

One useful exercise which illustrates this approach is the 'island game' (see Brandes and Phillips, 1978). Group members are given some basic resources, e.g. clay or plasticine, paper, crayons, twigs, pipe-cleaners, sellotape and asked to construct their fantasy island, without speaking. Still non-verbally, they are next asked to create their own place or home on the island. Finally, and now with talking allowed, they are requested to hold an island meeting to decide on their social organisation, bearing in mind the possibility of an external enemy arriving. This exercise illustrates many general and personal features of group life including non-verbal communication, the individual and the group, leadership, fight/flight, intimacy, boundaries, feeling alone, conflict and co-operation and so on. In the de-brief afterwards, members are asked to reflect on the extent to which the roles they adopted repeated their behaviour in 'real life' groups: there is often some similarity and an opportunity to gain insight in this way. It also provides a powerful reminder of the pressure new group members often face when trying to find their 'place' in a new group. Other useful exercises include 'stranded in the desert' (Johnson and Johnson, 1975), the 'Zin obelisk' (Woodcock, 1979) and simulations of groups making decisions. The advantage of using a range of exercises which require different skills and behaviours is that they help individuals to identify their own 'natural' style in groups, an essential starting point for group skills training.

Simulated experience of the groupworker role. This is a vital part of training which often gets omitted when practitioners are left to make the big leap from experiential group membership to designated leadership of a group for users. The essence of this training is creating group and groupwork scenarios, either fictional or reproductions of real groups, in which the trainee takes the worker or co-worker role. A video camera is used to film the simulation, which is then played back for critique, feedback and analysis. Worker skills and alternative approaches are practised and developed in this way. If video is not available, sound recordings can be used and also observers with specified briefs. The 'goldfish bowl' method of an outer circle observing an inner circle can be used with larger training groups. Simulations can also be devised to practise pre-group meetings and the group preparation stage when the social worker has to negotiate with colleagues and management to obtain the resources necessary to support a group project. When using these methods, it is important that peer feedback is offered constructively, which means acknowledging positives, being very specific about any criticisms and making practical suggestions for more effective group practice.

Using the literature　Practitioners learn in different ways and will use books, articles and training manuals to suit their personal approach. Some will prefer to read about it first and then try it out in practice, whereas others seem to prefer to experience group life first before they are motivated to delve into the literature. Relevant texts are referred to throughout this book, and appear in the bibliography at the end. Several training manuals have been produced in the last few years and a new one from the National Extension College (Henderson and Foster, 1991) is designed specifically for the trainers of group leaders/facilitators.

Learning through observing and doing　The trainee can learn much from the experienced groupworker through observing her or his practice, either directly when working with a group, through training films (see, for example, *Developing your Groupwork Skills*, Bristol University, 1986) or through written or spoken accounts of practice methods. It is essential however that the trainee develops her own style and skills at an early stage, and this means undertaking groupwork practice on training placements with skilled supervision. Experience of both working alone and with a co-worker should if possible be obtained at the formative stage. We shall now consider consultation and supervision, an important resource both for those new to groupwork and those who are more experienced.

Consultation and supervision

Two examples illustrate the potential value of consultation in groupwork. The first concerns two student social workers who were both quite inexperienced. They were on placement together and preparing to co-facilitate a group for people who had been quite recently bereaved and could benefit from meeting with others in a similar position. The two students had a consultation session with a tutor during the planning period, and they were obviously giving a lot of thought to all the practicalities of the arrangements and the proposed programme. After a while the consultant realised that they did not appear to be in touch with the likely feelings of the group members, and a group atmosphere which would inevitably be characterised by sadness, grieving and loss. They were asked if they had shared with each other their own feelings and experiences of death, grief and mourning, and their anticipated emotional response to this group: it transpired that quite unconsciously they had not even considered this fundamental aspect of their work together. This intervention by the consultant opened up the whole area of essential preparatory psychological work to be undertaken both individually and through honest sharing with each other, thus enabling them to be much better prepared for the sometimes very painful feelings that were to be expressed in the group.

The second example involved two quite experienced groupworkers, one male and one female. Their group was a multiple-families group with several families engaging in groupwork together, the common factor being that each family had one member who had been before the courts for an offence and was currently on probation. After one particularly difficult session the two workers were concerned about a problem they were experiencing in working together which was affecting their capacity to help this quite complex group. Each felt that their partner did not seem to have the same idea as they had about the direction in which the group session should be proceeding. A kind of tussle had developed between them in the group about how to proceed. They brought this problem to their consultant for assistance. As they talked about the issues the consultant built up a picture of two strong characters in conflict. On hunch he asked each of them to recollect previous groupwork pairings in which they had been involved, and the kind of role-relationship they had developed with their co-workers. Fascinatingly it transpired that each of them had always become the primary leader exercising overall control. They realised immediately that they had transferred this expectation to their partnership with each other, and not surprisingly were experiencing a power struggle! With this insight they made sure that they structured their future work together with the group on a basis which shared the leadership function equally, and this enabled the group to move forward more productively.

Groupwork is almost by definition a more complex activity than one-to-one casework because there are more variables to be considered. These include: each individual member of the group (up to 10 different people or more); sub-groupings; the group-as-a-whole; each worker and the co-working relationship; group purpose; the external environment; the programme; the setting; agency function; and most important of all the relationship betwen group task, group dynamics and group climate. Little wonder that groupworkers often 'hook into' particular group members or get caught up in the emotions and mood of the group, sometimes feeling all-powerful and at other times completely impotent. It is not easy to keep one's eyes on the task at the same time as concentrating on the experience of the group members collectively and individually, and coping with the feelings evoked in yourself.

It often helps to have a colleague as co-worker, but that in itself can create further difficulties if you get onto different wavelengths and feel isolated from each other. It is not easy for co-workers on their own to raise issues in their working relationship, but the presence of a third person often opens up communication about the difficult things. For all these reasons it can be a great help to have someone you can go to, to share the experience with and get assistance in sorting out what is happening and what to do next. This is why consultancy is such an important part of groupwork, especially for beginners but also for experienced workers when working with complex groups and new developments.

In this section we shall concentrate mostly on *consultation* which can occur with any 'helper' whatever his or her role may be in relation to the worker(s). We shall however also give brief consideration to groupwork *supervision* which usually occurs between a worker and his or her line-manager who holds the agency accountability for the service provided. The forum for consultation/supervision may be one-to-one (or one-to-two with co-workers) or some form of group consultation/supervision when several groupworkers working with different groups consult together in a group setting. For a more detailed treatment of consultation in general, or groupwork consultation in particular, see two of my other publications (A. Brown, 1984 and A. Brown, 1988 respectively). For an interesting discussion of various ways of relating groupwork to agency accountability see Manor (1989).

In successful consultation it is important that the consultee takes a proactive part in the proceedings. As in groupwork, people often start a new experience in a dependency mode and it is part of the responsibility of both the consultant and the consultee to ensure that a dynamic interactive relationship is established. The core principle is that the consultant enables the consultee to find her own way forward with assistance as appropriate. One of the pitfalls for the consultant is to get so involved that they in effect run the group by proxy through the influence and direction they exert on the consultee. In the long term this will do nothing for the latter's self-confidence and professional development.

The choice of consultant and the format for the consultancy sessions will depend on the purpose, type and focus of consultancy required. There is a basic distinction between *process consultancy*, which concentrates on what is happening between people, and *task consultancy*, which is concerned much more with the content and aims of the group. For example a co-worker pair facilitating a substance-abuse group may want help primarily with their own working relationship and the group dynamics (process) or primarily with substance-abuse issues (content). The former needs different kinds of consultancy skills from those required for the latter. There are experts on groups, experts on drugs, and a few who are expert on both! Splitting task and process in this way is of course a false dichotomy because the essence of groupwork skill lies in harnessing group process to group task. However, there can legitimately be a main emphasis on one or the other and this will influence consultancy arrangements.

Unlike a supervisor, who is the line-manager, a consultant can be drawn from any source within or external to the worker's agency. They usually have no formal accountability for the group and the service to users, their task being simply to try and enable the workers to work more effectively. Aside from the particular expertise of a potential consultant, other factors affecting choice will include: gender and race requirements (see Chapter 6); theoretical/values orientation; cost; acceptability to the agency, particularly if they are paying; and of course availability. Another factor which may be important is whether there is any history of either worker having any past involvement with the consultant. This may be an advantage or a disadvantage, and can be a complication when the consultant is well known to one of the workers but not to the other. If the consultancy goes ahead this initial imbalance in the relationship with the two workers needs to be acknowledged and worked through so it does not get in the way of productive work together.

Before a consultancy arrangement is confirmed a *contract* needs to be agreed between consultant and consultee(s) covering the main parameters of the work together including: the administrative nuts and bolts, e.g. time, length and place of meetings, fees where applicable; what prior sources of information if any will be available to the consultant (this can vary from nothing to background papers about the group, written records of group sessions, audio or video recordings, or possible live observation of the group); an understanding of how consultation agendas will be set or not set; the focus of consultancy sessions; methods to be used (will it all be verbal discussion or will experiential techniques be used?); confidentiality (what is the consultant's relationship with the employer, if any?); and any other important issues.

Consultancy varies greatly in the degree to which sessions are structured and organised in a set way. The following approach is recommended as one which combines a clear overall structure with maximum flexibility. It has the following stages:

– *preparation*   As with most things it pays to be well

prepared whether you are consultee or consultant. This means giving some thought to the session in advance, doing any preparatory reading and tuning-in at a feeling level.

- *joining* Basic to good communication is establishing the relationship anew and sensing the mood conveyed by the consultee(s). This is important because whilst it may be nothing to do with the group and connected with something quite different in the consultee's life, sometimes the way the consultant is made to feel gives clues as to how the group is making the worker feel – a form of unconscious mirroring.

- *constructing the agenda* There may be prearranged items or it may be an approach in which the agenda is formed 'on the spot'. The topics will initially be those raised by the consultee, although the consultant may sometimes make suggestions if it seems that something important is being missed. The items may need prioritising.

- *outlining the issues* The next phase is when the consultee outlines her concerns and the consultant's main task is to listen, perhaps seeking clarification of some points and empathising with what the consultee is expressing. When there are co-consultees the way they share the 'story' may say important things about how they are working together as well as giving information about the substantive issue. If the agreed agenda includes co-working issues it is important that each worker gets adequate space to present her or his experience and perspective.

- *discussing possible responses to 'the problem'* Not later than the halfway point is the time to shift the focus from 'problem-talking' to 'problem-solving', with the consultee first sharing her or his own ideas, and the consultant adding hers as appropriate. (*Note*: a purist view is that the consultant should never offer her own ideas or suggestions. This can be experienced as very withholding by the consultee, and I prefer a flexible approach provided the consultant is not directive and works mainly with what the consultee brings to the discussion.)

- *selection of a preferred strategy and method of implementation* This may occur during the session or may be something that the consultee(s) decides on later from a range of options considered during the consultation.

- *ending with some hope and optimism* As a general principle it is desirable that the consultee leaves the session feeling renewed competence and with some realistic optimism about the next stage of work with the group, whatever that may be.

Although the emphasis has been on consultancy, nearly everything discussed so far can be applied to consultation within the supervision relationship. The difference in a supervisory relationship is that both parties are aware of the power imbalance, which if there is not a strong basis of trust may inhibit the work, both through causing the consultee to be cautious and through 'contamination' by agendas which intrude from other dimensions of the supervisory relationship. A further complication may arise if the line-manager is not expert in groupwork and only offering consultation because of her role rather than knowledge, skills or interest. Nevertheless there are important aspects of accountability which have to be recognised and built in to the arrangements, particularly in statutory agencies.

Manor (1989), drawing on experiences shared by others at a workshop, conceptualises three ways in which accountability can be held other than by the line-manager being the consultant.

The first model, which Manor terms *parallel*, is the quite common situation when the group member's individual worker retains the 'allocated worker' role with line accountability to her supervisor, liaising as necessary with the groupworkers, who have their own consultant. The second model, referred to as *dual*, involves the allocation of all the group members to the two groupworkers facilitating their group. They then meet with other groupworkers in a group supervision group with two co-leaders, one offering consultancy on group process to all the groupworkers and groups represented, and the other, usually a line-manager carrying the agency accountability, intervening as appropriate when statutory or other agency-related supervisory issues arise.

The third approach is called *multiple accountability* and occurs when the groupworkers arrange a network of accountability involving all the workers from different agencies who are involved with each group member and their family. In the example written up by Shearer and Williment (1987) they received consultation for their work with the group and with the network from a consultant, and supervision on the accountability aspects from their team leader.

Manor indicates the advantages and disadvantages of each of these models, and encourages practitioners to continue developing imaginative ways of meeting their need for consultation, and the agency need for accountability. I think one of the reasons groupwork is not always popular with managers is because it is essentially a 'horizontal' approach and ethos whereas accountability for the delivery of services in statutory agencies is, perhaps necessarily, based on a bureaucratic 'vertical' model of control. The lesson from all this is that when groupwork consultation is arranged it is essential to tie it in with the agency system of accountability for the work done, in some mutually agreed way.

Group consultation and *group supervision* are surprisingly underused. This may be because rather more organisation is required than for one-to-one supervisory methods, just as in all forms of groupwork compared to one-to-one casework. In fact there are many similarities between group supervision and groupwork practice, and the key variables apply in the same way: for example, group size and composition; style of leadership; sharing group time equitably; degree of structure; focus on individual issues versus focus on common themes; confidentiality; stages of group development; mutual aid; issues of power and control.

One relatively simple structure for group approaches to consultation/supervision for, say, four pairs of co-workers with a facilitator, is to preplan for one or two groups to be covered in depth each session, with space at the beginning for joining and checking out 'hot' issues, and space at the end for any additional urgent matters. This model is described in more detail in Brown (1988, pp. 156–8). In a relatively homogeneous group the programme can be varied by theme-centred sessions: for example, if all consultees are working with groups in which there is potential or actual conflict between empowerment and control there might be much to share between groups, drawing on the consultees' different current experiences. The important thing is to be clear which model you are working to. If as consultee you regard your allocated group space as a special opportunity to get consultation on your group, major digressions into other group members' fascinating group experiences may not be very welcome! Aside from any time-saving advantages, one benefit of this group model – which should come naturally to groupworkers – is that all workers experience the peer consultant role in which their task is to facilitate the consultancy needs of colleagues, in the process learning more themselves.

Recording

Groupwork recording is more difficult than recording one-to-one interviews because of the complex nature of a small group. In groups with a task-oriented focus, recording will be concerned with tangible tasks, plans, actions and decisions. In a person-oriented group, where feelings, relationships and non-verbal communication receive high priority, recording is dealing with intangibles, perhaps the most difficult of all to write about. Most group records attempt to communicate both content and process.

Groupwork recording has several different purposes:

Agency requirements.　Most agencies require some written information on the official records about each piece of work done, particularly if it forms part of their statutory responsibilities. One difficulty is that records are usually designed for individual and family information, not group approaches. If the full group record appears in each individual's file there are problems of confidentiality as well as the difficulty of picking out the sections which are relevant to that individual. An alternative is to keep a separate group folder and to record only brief individual information in personal files, e.g. '18.11.91. John attended the group', or '18.11.91. Group meeting. John was involved in a fight when he arrived, but later showed real progress in co-operating with other boys to make a puppet stage.'

A confidentiality issue also arises when a group member is under the statutory supervision of a social worker not involved with the group. The group member (and the social worker) should know what kinds of information, if any, will be passed on to 'their' social worker, including what will be written down on their records. If a group folder approach is used, it raises interesting questions about where it is kept, and to whom it belongs – the groupworker, the group or the agency?

Training and skill development.   Detailed records, whether written or tape-recorded in sound or on video, are a key element in any groupwork training programme. Apart from their direct value to the practitioner in clarifying thoughts and feelings about a session, they provide material which can be available to the trainer or consultant for supervision sessions.

Planning, evaluation and research.   Some recording, however brief, of every group session or event facilitates assessment of individual and group progress, and programme planning. One of the main purposes is to have a record of changes over a period of time. This is often a surprise and encouragement to both the worker and group members themselves, who can easily underestimate the extent of progress over a period of months or even weeks. Systematic and planned recording is an essential part of any groupwork evaluation or research.

For direct use in work with group members.   A group record or diary may be kept, with different members taking responsibility for writing it up. The contents of the diary may be referred to and used as part of the programme. Periodic reference to this collective group record can also be a very useful way of monitoring and reviewing group progress. When you are in a group from week to week whether as member or worker it is easy to lose sight of the extent to which group progress has been achieved. The group record provides the evidence.

Users now have right of access to their personal records and these can be made easily available as a matter of policy. Individual group members can also be encouraged to write and keep their own personal record. The workers can give written feedback on both group and individual records, using that medium as another way of communicating with members. A very simple individual record which has been used successfully and can be adapted to different groups is given below.

Name: **Group:**   **Date:**

1.   Since the last group, what   ⎫   (To be completed
        have you done, or what   ⎪   before a session
        has happened that was   ⎬   starts.)
        important?   ⎪
                                        ⎪
2.   What are you hoping to   ⎪
        achieve at this meeting?   ⎭

3.   What have you achieved   ⎫   (To be completed
        at this meeting?   ⎬   at the end of the
                                        ⎪   session.)
                                        ⎪
4.   How do you feel about it?   ⎭

5.   Groupworker's notes   (To be added
        (feedback)   between sessions.)

(A section for peer feedback can be included if agreed in the group contract and treated as confidential.)

Written records.

The three media for recording are audio-tape, video-tape and written records. The group's permission is essential for the first two, with a clear understanding about who, if anyone, will have access to the tapes. This is made much easier if the tape is used subsequently in the group, so the members are involved with it rather than feeling something is being done to them, or taken away from them. Tapes are very useful for supervision purposes but also very time-consuming. As most groups have to rely on the written record, this is now considered in more detail.

Written records are not normally made during a group session, except when particular decisions need to be noted, perhaps about future programme plans. Unless the members are involved in the recording, the worker(s) will write it up afterwards. Co-workers can prearrange that one of them will be responsible, usually the one with the more secondary role in that session, though it does not always work out that way! It is important to make some brief notes as soon as possible after the meeting. As time passes, memory distorts and omits. The full version needs to have some structure to it, including scope for content and process.

In therapeutic/talking groups the clock or interaction chronogram (Cox, 1973) is sometimes used. This consists of a clock face with a circle for each participant, each circle being divided into three segments (see Fig. 7.1). Significant behaviour or achievement is written into each segment for each member. Arrows between members can be used to indicate the directions and quality of interactions.

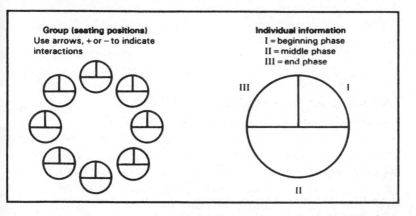

Fig. 7.1

A written outline, adaptable for most groups, to be completed by the worker or a designated member, can be made under the following headings:

1. Basic data to include date, venue, number of meeting, members and workers present/absent. (In a sedentary group, a clock-type map indicating seating positions can be useful.)

2. Plan for the session, as decided beforehand (perhaps referring to the group as a whole, individual members, workers).
3. Content, themes, activities, decisions (task emphasis).
4. Process, group interactions (relationship emphasis).
5. Individuals. Notes on each member's participation and progress.
6. Workers. Notes on worker/co-worker functioning.
7. Summary, linking what happened to aims and future plans.

Sections 3 and 4 are particularly difficult, especially in unstructured groups, because they are an attempt to communicate what actually happened in the group. The type of group and its aims, and the practitioner's own style, are likely to determine how the group is recorded. In the early stages more detail is needed, but at later stages it is changes and significant events which are particularly worth noting.

Evaluation

Evaluation of groupwork can be undertaken both formally and informally. It may be concerned with evaluating the effectiveness of a particular group method of intervention and/or with monitoring the contribution group participation has made to the achievement of each individual member's identified goals. The more formal type of evaluative groupwork research is relatively rare in the UK (but see Smith *et al.*, 1972; Caddick and Brown, 1982; Birrell-Weisen, 1991), and readers who are interested in the methodological issues are referred to Caddick (1983) and Dies (1978). Whitaker (1985, Chapter 6) demonstrates how 'by relatively little additional pre-planning and later work, the ordinary task of informal monitoring and assessment can be transformed into small-scale formal research'. What we are concerned with here is the responsibility which every practitioner has, in collaboration with users of services, to engage in regular evaluative efforts to try and find out what the social work intervention is achieving (outcome) and how it is being experienced (process).

Evaluation of the effectiveness of a group is an essential

part of the ending phase, but it should also be a recurrent theme during the group's life, as worker and group members review progress, and if necessary redefine goals and methods. Groupwork evaluation is complicated by the number of people involved, each with personal agendas. In many formed groups the progress of each individual is what counts, and the group approach is best assessed by the impact it has for each member. If, say, in a group of ten members, five achieve their goals, but five fail to achieve theirs, statements can be made about the effectiveness or otherwise of that group for each individual, but not so clearly overall. In a natural group, evaluation may be most significant at the group level if the goals are pitched at that level, e.g. 'to improve family members' communication with each other'. In a community group, evaluation could be in terms of some community change objective, such as the establishment of children's play facilities.

At whatever level evaluation is being used, it can only be meaningful if there has been some initial agreement or contract about goals and the means of trying to achieve them. The more specific the goals, the easier it will be to assess whether they have been achieved. This is not necessarily an argument for choosing very specific goals such as 'to smack my child not more than twice a week instead of every day', if less tangible goals like 'to feel more loving to my child' are needed. There is a balance to be struck between behaviourally specific and qualitatively significant goals.

Example: A support group for lone fathers with the general group aim of sharing experiences and ideas relating to managing a family single-handed. Within this general aim, more specific aims were identified as: developing a social life; caring for and controlling your children; discussing relationships with women, and remarriage; sorting out money problems. Each of these aims was different for each group member and had to be defined individually, e.g. for Fred 'to go out socially at least once every week' (easy to measure), or for Jim 'to cope better with my sixteen-year-old daughter's rebellious attitude' (less tangible and so more difficult to measure). More specific behaviour, e.g. 'to talk to her for half an hour without losing my temper' is possible but may over-simplify.

Having clarified *what* the goals are for each individual (and they may be changed or added to as the group develops and new needs emerge), the next question is *how* to assess whether the goals have been reached. This can be done by the individual themselves, the group, the worker, or all three. It is important that some part of the evaluation (of self, peers and the worker(s)) is written down as well as shared verbally in the group, because group pressures may inhibit individual statements. In addition to written and verbal evaluation at the end, written feedback can also be obtained several weeks or months after the group is over, when members may have a better perspective on the experience, and know whether any desired changes have been sustained. This can be done by sending each member a simple follow-up questionnaire (an s.a.e. improves the return rate!) or using structured follow-up interviews, with general questions about the group:

> *Example*: Before you came to the group, what did you expect it to be like? If you found it different from what you expected, in what ways was it different? Did you find the group very helpful/ quite helpful/rather unhelpful/very unhelpful?

and also more specific questions:

> *Example*: if you found the group helpful, can you say in what way it (a) helped you personally, (b) helped other group members? If you found the group unhelpful, can you say why?

Note: if writing things down is difficult for any group member, this should be identified at an early stage, and special arrangements made, for example to dictate answers to a friend or on to a tape.

Objective evaluation of groupwork effectiveness is difficult to achieve because of the complexity of the variables and problems of accurate measurement. The problems and possibilities of the 'scientific' approach are well illustrated in two recent accounts of attempts at using quantitative methods in groupwork evaluation (Birrell-Weisen, 1991; Cwikel and Oron, 1991). This should not deter the groupworker from rough-and-ready methods which obtain some useful information for future planning and agency policy. An awareness that you are expected to evaluate outcome makes you more likely to think carefully with participants at the beginning of a group about what they hope to achieve, and to set realistic, attainable goals.

Preston-Shoot (1988) suggests the following 'model for evaluation' which he illustrates with several practice examples:

Step 1: describe the current situation, as precisely as possible.

Step 2: describe the broad aim or desired outcome for the work.

Step 3: identify feasible objectives, specific goals, the achievement of which will help to achieve the desired situation.

Step 4: describe carefully the intervention designed to achieve the desired situation, including the methods to be used and the resources and time required.

Step 5: identify indicators (something observable which tells those involved that change or movement towards or away from an objective is occurring) which will reveal change.

Step 6: decide who will record what, how and when.

Step 7: set out the first six steps as a plan for evaluating the effect of the work, and implement it.

Step 8: establish and review the results of the intervention prior either to a return to step 1 or termination and subsequent follow-up. Set review dates at the beginning.

I would like to conclude this section on evaluation with a written account by a lone father of his experience in a lone fathers' group. It is not based on a set questionnaire or evaluation of specific goals, but is a moving account of what that group achieved for that person and for others, as he experienced it.

A group member's experience

'I joined the group only three months after becoming a single parent. In the space of literally a few weeks I had changed from being a reasonably happily married man to a wounded and confused single man with a small child to care for. My first concern was that the trauma for my son be minimised and so I gave up completely all efforts to work in order to maintain for him a settled and orderly home-life.

'Thus, when I joined the group it was as a man who unexpectedly had lost wife, lover, my son's mother, and career. The poignancy of this situation was highlighted in one fairly small aspect. In my work in caring for the mentally handicapped (sic) I had to handle supplementary benefit books for eight people, and every Monday morning signed and cashed about eight coupons for other people. Suddenly I was signing one for myself.

'Only those who have experienced it can understand the whirlwind of feelings that seem to overpower one completely at such times: rage, jealousy, longing, frustration, humiliation, loneliness, bitterness, fear, worry, all taking over from one another in a seemingly endless kaleidoscope. But the group helped: others had been there and others were still going through the same.

'From the first week one felt less alone. We exchanged household hints, where to get the cheapest children's clothes, how to save on fuel, how to save on food. I received tips on how to get a little bit more from the DHSS and rebates on electricity. For me this concentration on the practical and domestic helped to keep my feet rooted in each day.

'Other group members had to cope with far greater difficulties than I did and this put my problems into clearer perspective. I had a good flat. I had no disputes over property or custody. I had one amiable son whom I have been very close to since the day he was born. Others had problems that were monumental in comparison. One man had three children, one of whom was epileptic. Another had teenage daughters who completely baffled him. Another had spent his whole life rearing five children in cramped conditions.

'Some were a year or more past the worst of their crisis and could observe in us beginners patterns of thought and feeling they had experienced. This was a great comfort, to know that the violence of one's feelings would come and go but would eventually settle down.

'A major topic of discussion, and one returned to again and again, was of course children. Here I was far more confident as the rearing of my child was and is something that fits easily on my shoulders and so in this area I felt able to give something back to the group. One major fear, of course, and I think this was especially mine, was that our children would grow up with a distorted view of women. I found no answer to this worry. A lasting impression from these discussions was that this was the most important factor for consideration. Anyone who thinks men cannot, because they are men, bring up children and all the problems they bring and find fulfilment in the experience, would have been enlightened if they had heard these conversations.

'As is to be expected, there was much discussion of women and this was at times quite naturally very distorted. Some of the group tried to balance this by keeping in mind that their experience of women was not to be projected on to all women. Others were immovably of the opinion that all women were reckless, lazy, completely unable to bear responsibility and that marriage was a waste of effort. These discussions were important. I was attracted to women. I had been deeply wounded by a woman and so in a turmoil of attraction and defensive rejection, I was then going rapidly from woman to woman perhaps out of loneliness, perhaps out of revenge, probably both. So it was important to me to bring out into the open my feelings lest this destructive pattern go on endlessly.

'Some members of the group felt we should meet and talk with single mothers. Some of us disagreed and I still do, although perhaps now I would reserve that opinion for those who are recently single and in a highly emotional state. It would be quite helpful, I am sure, to talk with women as single parents and householders when we were adjusted to that status. But to be in a mixed group at a time when we were still wounded lovers would have great dangers, I think, for many of our feelings about the opposite sex were very confused. I found the exclusive company of men in this group of great comfort. I think now, after a year has passed, a mixed group would not hold dangers.

'When I first went to the group I decided beforehand that if I were going to spend the evening amongst a roomful of moaning, self-pitying men, I would only attend once. Nothing impressed me more than our determination to stay afloat and maintain our self-respect. This was, I think, why some of us had no wish to carry on with the group more than the seven weeks. Our status as fathers alone could become our identity and the centre of our approach to life.

'For myself, I have now no wish to make special formal contact with other single parents, but in the midst of my crisis months, the support and help of this group was invaluable and so if at any time my experience could help others, I would be only too glad to participate again.'

(I would like to thank the former group member for this generous contribution. He prefers to remain anonymous.)

Bibliography

Note: (i) The bibliography includes all the references made in the book. A selection of these have been asterisked (*). They are basic texts and articles which between them offer the reader a comprehensive foundation in groupwork theory and skills.

       (ii) SWG refers to the journal *Social Work with Groups*.

Alissi, A. and Casper, M. (eds, 1985), 'Time as a Factor in Groupwork: Time-Limited Groupwork Experiences', *SWG*, 8(2).

Anstey, M. (1982), 'Scapegoating in Groups: Some Theoretical Perspectives and a Case Record of Intervention', *SWG*, 5(3).

Aplin, G. (1977), 'Some Thoughts on Teaching the Design and Evaluation of Groupwork Practice', in N. McCaughan and K. McDougall (eds), *Group Work – A Guide for Teachers and Practitioners*, NISW Paper No. 7.

Atherton, J.S. (1986), *Professional Supervision in Group Care* (London, Tavistock).

Atkinson, D. (1989), 'Group Homes for People with Mental Handicap: Key Issues for Everyday Living' in A. Brown and R. Clough (eds, 1989), *Groups and Groupings* (London, Tavistock/Routledge).

Badham, B., Bente, M. and Hall, P. (1988), 'Nowt to Do and Always Getting into Trouble', *Groupwork*, 1(3).

Bales, R.F. (1950), *Interaction Process Analysis* (Reading, Mass., Addison-Wesley).

Ball, L. and Sowa, T. (1985), *Groupwork and I.T.* (London Intermediate Treatment Association).

Ball, L. and Sowa, T. (1989), 'Groupwork in Intermediate

Treatment' in A. Brown and R. Clough (eds), *Groups and Groupings: Life and Work in Day and Residential Centres* (London, Tavistock/Routledge).

Bazalgette, J. (1971), *Freedom, Authority and the Young Adult* (London, Pitman).

*Benson, J. (1987), *Working Creatively with Groups* (London, Tavistock).

Bernard, L., Burton, J., Kyne, P. and Simon, J. (1988), 'Groups for Older People in Residential and Day Care: The Other Groupworkers', *Groupwork*, 1(2).

Bernstein, S. (1972), 'Values and Group Work', in S. Bernstein (ed.), *Further Explorations in Group Work* (London, Bookstall Publications).

*Bertcher, H. and Maple, F. (1977), *Creating Groups* (London, Sage Publications).

Birrell-Weisen, R. (1991), 'Evaluative Study of Groupwork for Stress and Anxiety', *Groupwork*, 4(2).

Blatner, H. (1973), *Acting-In: Practical Applications of Psycho-dramatic Methods* (Springer Publishing Company, Inc.)

Bodinham, H. and Weinstein, J. (1991), 'Making Authority Accountable: The Experience of a Statutory-based Women's Group', *Groupwork*, 4(1).

Bond, T. (1986), *Games for Social and Life Skills* (London, Hutchinson).

Boushel, M. (1991), 'Anti-Discriminatory Work on Placement: Helping Students Prepare', *Social Work Education*, 10(3), 60–78.

Brandes, D. (1982), *Gamesters 2* (London, Hutchinson).

*Brandes, D. and Phillips, H. (1978), *Gamesters' Handbook* (London, Hutchinson).

*Breton, M. (1985), 'Reaching and Engaging People: Issues and Practice Principles', *SWG*, 8(3).

Breton, M. (1990), 'Learning from Social Groupwork Traditions', *SWG*, 13(3).

Breton, M. (1991), 'Toward a Model of Social Groupwork Practice with Marginalised Populations', *Groupwork*, 4(1).

Brimelow, M. and Wilson, J. (1982), 'A Problem Shared', 'Drawing the Circle', 'Ourselves Alone', *Social Work Today*, 13(19, 20, 21).

Briscoe, C. (1978), 'Programme Activities in Social Group

Work', in N. McCaughan (ed.), *Group Work: Learning and Practice* (London, George Allen and Unwin).

Bristol University (1986), *Developing Your Groupwork Skills*, Skills Training Videotape (97 mins).

Brower, A., Garvin, C., Hobson, J., Reed, B. and Reed, H. (1987), 'Exploring the Effects of Leader Gender and Race on Group Behaviour' in J. Lassner, K. Powell and E. Finnigan (eds, 1987), *Social Groupwork: Competence and Values in Practice* (New York, Haworth Press).

Brown, A. (1977), 'Worker-style in Social Work', *Social Work Today*, 8(29).

Brown, A. (1979 and 1986 edns), *Groupwork* (Aldershot, Gower).

Brown, A. (1984), *Consultation* (London, Heinemann).

Brown, A. (1988), 'Consultation for Groupworkers: Models and Methods', *SWG*, 11(1/2), 145–163.

Brown, A. (1990), 'Groupwork with a Difference: The Group "Mosaic" in Residential and Day Centre Settings', *Groupwork*, 3(3).

*Brown, A., Caddick, B., Gardiner, M. and Sleaman, S. (1982), 'Towards a British Model of Groupwork', *British Journal of Social Work*, 12(6), 587–605.

Brown, A. and Caddick, B. (eds, 1991), *Groupwork with Offenders*, special issue *Groupwork*, 4(3).

*Brown, A. and Clough, R. (eds, 1989), *Groups and Groupings: Life and Work in Day and Residential Centres* (London and New York, Tavistock/Routledge).

Brown, A. and Seymour, B. (eds, 1983), *Intake Groups for Clients: A Probation Innovation*, (School of Advanced Urban Studies, University of Bristol).

Brown, C. (1986), *Child Abuse Parents Speaking* (School of Advanced Urban Studies, University of Bristol).

Brown, J.A. (1984), 'Group Work with Low-income Black Youths', *SWG*, 7(3).

Burnham, J. (1986), *Family Therapy* (London, Tavistock).

Burton, J. (1989), 'Institutional Change and Group Action: The Significance and Influence of Groups in Developing New Residential Services for Older People', in A. Brown and R. Clough (eds, 1989), *Groups and Groupings* (London, Tavistock/Routledge).

*Butler, S. and Wintram, C. (1991), *Feminist Groupwork* (London, Sage Publications).

*Button, L. (1974), *Developmental Group Work with Adolescents* (London, University of London Press).

Caddick, B. (1983), 'Intake Group Evaluation' in A. Brown and B. Seymour (eds), *Intake Groups for Clients*, (School of Advanced Urban Studies, University of Bristol).

Caddick, B. (1991), 'The Use of Groups in Working with Offenders', *Groupwork*, 4(3).

Caddick, B. and Brown, A. (1982), 'The Problems and Promise of Evaluating Practice: A Groupwork Example', *Probation*, December 1982.

Carter, J. (1988), *Creative Day-Care for Mentally Handicapped People* (Oxford, Blackwell).

Cartwright, D. and Zander, A. (eds, 1968), *Group Dynamics: Research and Theory* (New York, Harper and Row).

Chau, K. (1990a), 'Social Work with Groups in Multicultural Contexts', *Groupwork*, 3(1).

*Chau, K. (ed., 1990b), *Ethnicity and Biculturalism: Emerging Perspectives of Social Group Work*, special issue *SWG*, 13(4).

Clarke, P. and Aimable, A. (1990), 'Groupwork Techniques in a Residential Primary School for Emotionally Disturbed Boys', *Groupwork*, 3(1).

Clerkin, E. and Knaggs, B. (1991), 'Working Creatively with Children', *Groupwork*, 4(1).

Clough, R. (1981), *Old Age Homes* (London, George Allen and Unwin).

Clough, R. (1982), *Residential Work* (Basingstoke, Macmillan).

Comaz-Diaz, L. (1984), 'Content Themes in Group Treatment with Puerto Rican Women', *SWG*, 7(3).

Cooper, J. (1980), *Social Groupwork with Elderly People in Hospital* (Stoke-on-Trent, Beth Johnson Foundation).

Cowburn, M. (1990), 'Work with Male Sex Offenders in Groups', *Groupwork*, 3(2).

Cox, M. (1973), 'The Group Therapy Interaction Chronogram', *British Journal of Social Work*, 3(2).

Craig, R. (1988), 'Structured Activities with Adolescent Boys', *Groupwork*, 1(1).

Cressey, D.R. (1955), 'Changing Criminals: The Application of the Theory of Differential Association', *American Journal of Sociology*.

Croxton, T. (1974), 'The Therapeutic Contract in Social Treatment', in P. Glasser, R. Sarri and R. Vinter (eds), *Individual Change Through Small Groups* (New York, The Free Press).

Cwikel, J. and Oron, A. (1991), 'A Long-term Support Group for Chronic Schizophrenic Outpatients: A Quantitative and Qualitative Evaluation', *Groupwork*, 4(2).

*Davies, B. (1975), *The Use of Groups in Social Work Practice* (London, Routledge and Kegan Paul).

Davis, L. (1980), 'Racial Balance – A Psychological Issue', *SWG*, 3(2).

Davis, L. (1984), 'Essential Components of Group Work with Black Americans', *SWG*, 7(3).

*Davis, L. and Proctor, E. (1989), *Race, Gender and Class: Guidelines for Individuals, Families and Groups* (New Jersey, Prentice Hall).

Dearling, A. and Armstrong, H. (1984), *The Youth Games Book* (Renfrewshire, I.T.Resource Centre).

Delgado, M. and Humm-Delgado, D. (1984), 'Hispanics and Groupwork: A Review of the Literature', *SWG*, 7(3).

Derricourt, N. and Penrose, J. (1984), 'Groupwork with Young Offenders: Working out a Theory for Practice', *Social Work Education*, 4(1).

DeVere, M. and Rhonne, O. (1991), 'The Use of Photographs as a Projective and Facilitative Technique in Groups', *Groupwork*, 4(2).

Dies, R.R. (ed., 1978), 'Symposium on Therapy and Encounter Group Research', *Small Group Behaviour*, 9(2).

Dies, R.R. and Cohen, (1976), 'Content Considerations in Group Therapist Disclosure', *International Journal of Group Psychotherapy*, 1976.

*Donnelly, A. (1986), *Feminist Social Work with a Women's Group*, Social Work Monographs 41, University of East Anglia, Norwich.

Douglas, T. (1970), *A Decade of Small Group Theory, 1960–70* (London: Bookstall Publications).

*Douglas, T. (1976), *Groupwork Practice* (London, Tavistock Publications).

Douglas, T. (1978), *Basic Groupwork* (London, Tavistock Publications).

Douglas, T. (1983), *Groups: Understanding People Gathered Together* (London: Tavistock Publications).

Douglas, T. (1986), *Group Living: The Application of Group Dynamics in Residential Settings* (London, Tavistock).

*Douglas, T. (1991), *A Handbook of Common Groupwork Problems* (London, Tavistock/Routledge).

Edwards, E.D. and Edwards, M.E. (1984), 'Group Work Practice with American Indians', *SWG*, 7(3).

*Engebrigtsen, G.E. and Heap, K. (1988), 'Short-term Groupwork in the Treatment of Chronic Sorrow: A Norwegian Experience', *Groupwork*, 1(3).

*Ernst, S. and Goodison, L. (1982), *In our own Hands: A Book of Self-Help Therapy* (London, The Women's Press).

Ernst, S. and McGuire, M. (eds, 1987), *Living with the Sphinx: Papers from the Women's Therapy Centre* (London, Women's Press).

Fiedler, F.E. (1967), *A Theory of Leadership Effectiveness* (New York, McGraw-Hill).

Freeman, E.M. and McRoy, R. (1986), 'Group Counselling Program for Unemployed Black Teenagers', *SWG*, 9(1).

French, J.R.P. and Raven, P. (1967), 'The Bases of Social Power' in D. Cartwright (ed.), *Studies in Social Power* (Ann Arbor, Mich., Institute for Social Research).

Fulcher, L.C. and Ainsworth, F. (1985), *Group Care Practice with Children* (London, Tavistock).

Gale, D. (1990), *What is Psychodrama?* (Loughton: Gale Centre Publications).

*Galinsky, M.J. and Schopler, J.H. (1977), 'Warning: Groups may be Dangerous', *Social Work*, March 1977.

Galinsky, M.J. and Schopler, J.H. (1980), 'Structuring Co-leadership in Social Work Training', *SWG*, 3(4).

*Galinsky, M.J. and Schopler, J.H. (1985), 'Patterns of Entry and Exit in Open-ended Groups', *SWG*, 8(2).

Garland, J.A., Jones, H.E. and Kolodny, R.L. (1965), 'A Model for Stages of Development in Social Work with Groups' in S. Bernstein (ed.), *Explorations in Groupwork* (Boston, University School of Social Work).

*Garland, J.A. and Kolodny, R.L. (1972), 'Characteristics and Resolution of Scapegoating', in S. Bernstein (ed.),

Further Explorations in Groupwork (London, Bookstall Publications).

Garvin, C. (1974), 'Group Process: Uses and Usage in Social Work Practice' in P. Glasser, R. Sarri and R. Vinter (eds), *Individual Change in Small Groups* (New York, The Free Press).

*Garvin, C. (1981), *Contemporary Groupwork* (Englewood Cliffs, N.J., Prentice Hall).

*Garvin, C. and Reed, B. (eds, 1983), *Groupwork with Women/Groupwork with Men*, special issue of *SWG*, 6(3/4).

Garvin, C., Reid, W. and Epstein, L. (1976), 'A Task-Centred Approach' in R. Roberts and H. Northen (eds), *Theories of Social Work with Groups* (New York, Columbia University Press).

Getzel, G.S. and Mahony, K.F. (1989), 'Confronting Human Finitude: Groupwork with People with Aids', *Groupwork*, 2(2).

*Glasser, P., Sarri, R. and Vinter, R. (eds, 1974), *Individual Change Through Small Groups* (New York, The Free Press).

Glasser, W. (1965), *Reality Therapy* (New York, Harper and Row).

*Goldstein, H. (1988), 'A Cognitive-humanistic/Social Learning Perspective on Social Groupwork Practice', *SWG*, 11(1/2).

Gordon, K. (1992), 'Improving Groupwork Practice Through Illuminative Evaluation', *Groupwork*, 5(1).

Gorrell-Barnes, G. (1984), *Working with Families* (Basingstoke, Macmillan).

Green, R. (1987), 'Racism and the Offender: A Probation Response' in J. Harding (ed., 1987), *Probation and the Community* (London, Tavistock).

*Habermann, U. (1990), 'Self-help Groups: A Minefield for Professionals', *Groupwork*, 3(3).

Hall, E.T. (1969), *The Hidden Dimension* (New York, Doubleday).

Hankinson, I. and Stephens, D. (1985), 'In and Out of Context', *Community Care*, 4.7.85.

Hanmer, J. and Statham, D. (1988), *Women and Social Work: Towards a Woman-Centred Practice* (London, Macmillan).

Hare, A.P. (1962), *Handbook of Small Group Research* (New York, The Free Press).

*Hartford, M. (1971), *Groups in Social Work* (New York, Columbia U.P.).

Hawkins, P. (1989), 'The Social Learning Approach to Residential and Day Care' in A. Brown and R. Clough (eds, 1989), *Groups and Groupings* (London, Tavistock/ Routledge).

Heap, K. (1977), *Group Theory for Social Workers* (Oxford, Pergamon).

*Heap, K. (1979), *Process and Action in Social Work with Groups* (Oxford, Pergamon).

*Heap, K. (1985), *The Practice of Social Work with Groups* (London, George Allen & Unwin.

Heap, K. (1988), 'The Worker and the Group Process: A Dilemma Revisited', *Groupwork*, 1(1).

Heap, K. (ed., 1989), 'Groupwork in Europe', *Groupwork*, special issue 2(3).

*Henderson, P. and Foster, G. (1991), *Groupwork Skills Pack* (Cambridge, National Extension College).

*Henry, M. (1988), 'Revisiting Open Groups' *Groupwork*, 1(3).

Henry, S. (1981), *Group Skills in Social Work,* (U.S.A, F.E. Peacock).

Hil, R. (1986), 'Centre 81: Clients' and Officers' Views on the Southampton Day Centre' in J. Pointing (ed., 1986), *Alternatives to Custody* (Oxford, Blackwell).

Hodge, J. (1977), 'Social Groupwork: Rules for Establishing the Group', *Social Work Today*, 8(17), 1.2.77.

*Hodge, J. (1985), *Planning for Co-leadership*, Grapevine, 43 Fern Ave, Newcastle-Upon-Tyne, NE2 2QU.

*Houston, G. (1984 and 1990a), *The Red Book of Groups* (London, The Rochester Foundation).

Houston, G. (1990b), *The Red Book of Gestalt* (London, The Rochester Foundation).

Jennings, S. (1973), *Remedial Drama* (London, Pitman).

Jennings, S. (ed., 1987), *Dramatherapy* (London, Croom Helm).

*Johnson, D.W. and Johnson, F.P. (1975), *Joining Together: Group Theory and Group Skills* (Englewood Cliffs, N.J., Prentice-Hall).

Jones, M. (1953), *The Therapeutic Community* (New York, Basic Books).

Jones, M., Mordecai, M., Rutter, F. and Thomas, L. (1991), 'The Miskin Model of Groupwork with Women Offenders', *Groupwork*, 4(3).

Jones, R. and Kerslake, A. (1979), *Intermediate Treatment and Social Work* (London, Heinemann Educational Books).

Kemp, T. and Taylor, A. (1990), *The Groupwork Pack* (London, Longman).

*Kerslake, A. and Brown, A. (eds, 1990), *Child Sexual Abuse: The Groupwork Response*, special issue of *Groupwork*, 3(2).

Kesey, K. (1973), *One Flew Over the Cuckoo's Nest* (London, Pan Books, Picador).

Kingston. P. and Smith, D. (1983), 'Preparation for Live Consultation and Live Supervision', *Journal of Family Therapy*, 5, 219–233.

*Konopka, G. (1983), *Social Groupwork: A Helping Process*, 3rd edn (Englewood Cliffs, N.J., Prentice-Hall).

Kreeger, L. (ed., 1975), *The Large Group* (London, Constable, and Maresfield reprints).

Krzowski, S. and Land, P. (eds, 1988), *In our Experience* (London, Women's Press).

Laming, H. and Sturton, S. (1978), 'Group Work in a Social Services Department' in N. McCaughan (ed.), *Group Work: Learning and Practice* (London, George Allen & Unwin).

Lang, N. (1972), 'A Broad-Range Model of Practice in the Social Work Group', *Social Service Review*, 46, 76–89.

Lang, N. (1986), 'Social Work Practice in Small Social Forms' in N. Lang (ed.), *Collectivity in Social Groupwork: Concept and Practice*, SWG, special issue 9(4).

Langan, M. and Lee, P. (eds, 1989), *Radical Social Work Today* (London, Unwin Hyman).

*Lee, J. (1991), 'Empowerment Through Mutual Aid Groups: A Practice Grounded Conceptual Framework', *Groupwork*, 4(1).

Lennox, D. (1982), *Residential Group Therapy for Children* (London, Tavistock Publications).

Levinson, D. and Astrachan, B. (1976), 'Entry into the Mental Health Centre – A Problem in Organisational

Boundary Regulation' in E. Miller (ed., 1976), *Task and Organisation* (London, Wiley).

Lieberman, M.A., Yalom, I.D. and Miles, M.B. (1973), *Encounter Groups: First Facts* (New York, Basic Books).

Liebmann, M. (1986), *Art Therapy for Groups* (Beckenham, Croom Helm).

Lippitt, R. and White, R.K. (1953), 'Leader Behaviour and Member Reaction in Three Different Climates' in D. Cartwright and A. Zander (eds, 1968), *Group Dynamics*, 3rd edn (New York, Harper and Row).

McCaughan, N. (1977), 'Group Behaviour: Some Theories for Practice' in C. Briscoe and D.N. Thomas (eds), *Community Work: Learning and Supervision* (London, George Allen & Unwin.

*McCaughan, N. (ed., 1978), *Group Work: Learning and Practice* (London, George Allen & Unwin).

McCaughan, N. (1985), 'Groupwork Going Great Guns' *Social Work Today*, 22.7.85.

McGuire, J. and Priestley, P. (1981), *Life After School* (Oxford, Pergamon).

McLeod, L.W. and Pemberton, B.K. (1987), 'Men Together in Group Therapy' in F. Abbott (ed., 1987), *New Men, New Minds* (The Crossing Press).

Mackintosh, J. (1991), 'The Newcastle Intensive Probation Programme: A Centralised Approach to Groupwork', *Groupwork*, 4(3).

Manor, O. (1986), 'The Preliminary Interview in Social Groupwork: Finding the Spiral Steps', *SWG*, 9(2).

*Manor, O. (1988), 'Preparing the Client for Social Groupwork' *Groupwork*, 1(2).

Manor, O. (1989), 'Organising Accountability for Social Groupwork: More Choices', *Groupwork*, 2(2).

Maple, F. (1977), *Shared Decision Making* (New York, Sage Publications).

Masson, H. and Erooga, M. (1990), 'The Forgotten Parent: Groupwork with Mothers of Sexually Abused Children', *Groupwork*, 3(2).

Middleman, R. (1980), 'The Use of Program – review and update' *SWG*, 3(3).

Mistry, T. (1989), 'Establishing a Feminist Model of Groupwork in the Probation Service', *Groupwork*, 2(2).

Mistry, T. (1991), personal communication.

*Mistry, T. and Brown, A. (1991), 'Black/white Co-working in Groups', *Groupwork*, 4(2).

Mullender, A. (1988), 'Groupwork as the Method of Choice with Black Children in White Foster Homes', *Groupwork*, 1(2).

*Mullender, A. and Ward, D. (1991), *Self-Directed Groupwork: Users Take Action for Empowerment* (London, Whiting and Birch).

*Muston, R. and Weinstein, J. (1988), 'Race and Groupwork: Some Experiences in Practice and Training', *Groupwork*, 1(1).

Palmer, B. (1978), 'Fantasy and Reality in Group Life: A Model for Learning by Experience', in N. McCaughan (ed., 1978), *Groupwork: Learning and Practice* (London, George Allen & Unwin).

Palmer, T.B. (1973), 'Matching Worker and Client in Corrections', *Social Work*, 18(2).

*Papell, C. and Rothman, B. (1966), 'Social Groupwork Models: Possession and Heritage', *Journal for Education for Social Work*, 2(2), 66–77. Reprinted in H. Specht and A. Vickery (eds, 1977), *Integrated Social Work Methods* (London, George Allen & Unwin).

*Papell. C. and Rothman, B. (1980), 'Relating the Mainstream Model of Social Work with Groups to Group Psychotherapy and the Structured Group', *SWG*, 3(2).

Parloff, M. and Dies, R. (1977), 'Group Psychotherapy Outcome Research, 1966–75', *International Journal of Group Psychotherapy*, July 1977.

Parsloe, P. (1981), *Social Services Area Teams* (London, George Allen & Unwin).

Paulson, I., Burroughs, J.C. and Gelb, C.B. (1976), 'Co-therapy: What is the Crux of the Relationship', *The International Journal of Group Psychotherapy*, 1976.

Payne, C. (1978), 'Working with Groups in the Residential Setting' in N. McCaughan (ed.), *Group Work: Learning and Practice* (London, George Allen & Unwin).

Pearson, V. (1991), 'Western Theory, Eastern Practice: Social Group Work in Hong Kong', *SWG*, 14(2).

Perls, F. (1971), *Gestalt Therapy Verbatim* (New York, Bantam Books).

Phillips, J. (1989), 'Targeted Group Activities in Group Contexts', *Groupwork*, 2(1).

Pirsig, R.M. (1976), *Zen and the Art of Motor-Cycle Maintenance* (London, Corgi).

Pitman, E. (1984), *Transactional Analysis for Social Workers and Counsellors* (London, Routledge and Kegan Paul).

Pointing, J. (ed., 1986), *Alternatives to Custody* (Oxford, Blackwell).

*Preston-Shoot, M. (1987), *Effective Groupwork* (London, Macmillan).

*Preston-Shoot, M. (1988), 'A Model for Evaluating Groupwork', *Groupwork*, 1(2), 147–157.

Preston-Shoot, M. (1989), 'Using Contracts in Groupwork', *Groupwork*, 2(1), 36–47.

*Priestley, P. and McGuire, J. *et al.* (1978), *Social Skills and Personal Problem Solving* (London, Tavistock).

Reddin, W.J. (1970), *Managerial Effectiveness* (New York, McGraw-Hill).

Redl, F. (1951), 'Art of Group Composition' in S. Shulze (ed.), *Creative Living in a Children's Institution* (New York, Association Press).

*Reed, B.G. and Garvin, C. (eds, 1983), *Groupwork with Women/Groupwork with Men*, SWG, 6(3/4), special issue (Haworth Press).

Reid, K. (1988), 'But I Don't Want to Lead a Group', *Groupwork*, 1(2).

*Rhule, C. (1988), 'A Group for White Women with Black Children', *Groupwork*, 1(1).

Roberts, R.W. and Northen, H. (eds, 1976), *Theories of Social Work with Groups* (New York, Columbia U.P.).

Roman, M. (1976), 'Symposium: Family Therapy and Group Therapy – Similarities and Differences', *International Journal of Group Psychotherapy*.

*Rose, S. (1978), *Group Therapy: A Behavioural Approach* (Englewood Cliffs, N.J., Prentice-Hall).

Rose, S. (ed., 1980), *A Casebook in Group Therapy* (Englewood Cliffs, N.J., Prentice-HalL).

Ross, R.R., Fabiano, E. and Ross, R.D. (1986), *Reasoning and Rehabilitation: A Handbook for Teaching Cognitive Skills* (Ottawa, Cognitive Centre).

Ross, S. (1991), 'The Termination Phase in Social Groupwork: Tasks for the Groupworker', *Groupwork*, 4(1).

*Ross, S. and Bilson, A. (1981), 'The Sunshine Group: An

Example of Social Work Intervention Through the Use of a Group', *SWG*, 4(1/2).

Ross, S. and Thorpe, A. (1988), 'Programming Skills in Social Groupwork', *Groupwork*, 1(2).

Sainsbury, E. (1975), *Social Work with Families* (London, Routledge & Kegan Paul).

Sarri, R. and Galinsky, M.J. (1974), 'A Conceptual Framework for Group Development' in P. Glasser, R. Sarri and R. Vinter (eds), *Individual Change Through Small Groups* (New York, The Free Press).

*Schopler, J.H. and Galinsky, M. (1984), 'Meeting Practice Needs: Conceptualising the Open-ended Group', *SWG*, 7(2).

Schutz, W.C. (1958), *FIRO. – A Three-Dimensional Theory of Interpersonal Behaviour* (New York, Rinehart).

*Schwartz, W. (1971), 'On the Use of Groups in Social Work Practice' in W. Schwartz and S.R. Zalba, *The Practice of Group Work* (New York, Columbia U.P.).

*Shaffer, J.B.P. and Galinsky, M.D. (1974), *Models of Group Therapy and Sensitivity Training* (Englewood Cliffs, N.J., Prentice-Hall).

Shah, N. (1989), 'It's up to you Sisters: Black Women and Radical Social Work' in M. Langan and P. Lee (eds, 1989), *Radical Social Work Today* (London, Unwin Hyman).

*Shaw, M.E. (1976), *Group Dynamics* (New York, McGraw-Hill).

Shearer. P. and Williment, S. (1987), 'Taking a Risk: Groupwork with Families at Risk', *Practice*, 1, 15–26.

Sherif, M. and Sherif, C.W. (1969), *Social Psychology* (New York, Harper & Row).

Shulman, L. (1978), 'A Study of Practice Skills', *Social Work*, 23(4).

*Shulman, L. (1984 edn), *The Skills of Helping: Individuals and Groups* (F.E. Peacock).

Silverman, P. (1980), *Mutual Help Groups* (London, Sage).

Slater, P.E. (1958), 'Contrasting Correlates by Group Size' *Sociometry*, XXI, 129–139.

Slavson, S.R. (1943), *An Introduction to Group Therapy* (New York, International Universities Press Inc.).

*Smith, C.S., Farrant, M.R. and Marchant, H.J. (1972), *The Wincroft Youth Project* (London, Tavistock).

Smith, P. (1978), 'Group Work as a Process of Social Influence' in N. McCaughan (ed., 1978), *Group Work: Learning and Practice* (London, George Allen & Unwin).

*Smith, P. (1980), *Group Processes and Personal Change* (New York, Harper and Row).

Smith, P. (1985), 'Group Process Methods of Intervention in Race Relations' in J. Shaw, P.G. Noordlie *et al.* (eds, 1985), *Strategies for Improving Race Relations* (Manchester University Press).

Solomon, B.B. (1976), *Black Empowerment: Social Work in Oppressed Communities* (New York, Columbia).

Stephenson, R.M. and Scarpitti, F.R. (1974), *Group Interaction as Therapy* (U.S.A., Greenwood Press).

Stevenson, O., Parsloe, P. *et al.* (1978), *Social Service Teams: The Practitioner's View* (London, HMSO, for the DHSS).

Stodgill, R.M. (1948), 'Personal Factors Associated with Leadership: A Survey of the Literature', *Journal of Psychology*, 25, 35–71.

Stones, C. (1989), 'Groups and Groupings in a Family Centre' in A. Brown and R. Clough (eds, 1989), *Groups and Groupings* (London, Tavistock/Routledge).

Sulman, J. (1986), 'The Worker's Role in Collectivity', *SWG*, 9(4).

Thomas, D. (1986), *White Bolts, Black Locks* (London, Allen & Unwin).

Thomas, D.N. (1978), 'Journey into the Acting Community: Experiences of Learning and Change in Community Groups' in N. McCaughan (ed.), *Group Work: Learning and Practice* (London, George Allen & Unwin).

Thomas, E.J. (1967), 'Themes in Small Group Theory' in E.J. Thomas (ed.), *Behavioural Science for Social Workers* (New York, The Free Press).

Todd, T. and Barcombe, J. (1980), 'Use of Groups at Intake: Impact upon Clients, Staff and Program', *SWG*, 3(3).

Treacher, A. and Carpenter, J. (eds, 1984), *Using Family Therapy* (Oxford, Basil Blackwell).

Tribe, R. and Shackman, J. (1989), 'A Way Forward: A Group for Refugee Women' *Groupwork*, 2(2).

*Triseliotis, J. (ed., 1988), *Groupwork in Adoption and Foster Care* (London, Batsford).

Truax, C. and Carkhuff, R. (1967), *Towards Effective Counselling and Psychotherapy: Training and Practice* (Chicago, Aldine).

*Tuckman, B.W. (1965), 'Developmental Sequence in Small Groups', *Psychological Bulletin*, 63(6), 384–99.

Vanstone, M. (1986), 'The Pontypridd Day-training Centre: Diversion from Prison in Action' in J. Pointing (ed., 1986), *Alternatives to Custody* (Oxford, Blackwell).

Vinter, R. (1974), 'Program Activities: An Analysis of their Effects on Participant Behaviour' in P. Glasser, R. Sarri and R. Vinter (eds), *Individual Change Through Small Groups* (New York, The Free Press).

Vorrath, H.H. and Brendtro, L.K. (1984 edn), *Positive Peer Culture* (Chicago, Aldine).

Walker, L. (1978), 'Work with a Parents' Group' in N. McCaughan (ed.), *Groupwork: Learning and Practice* (London, George Allen & Unwin).

Ward, D. (1990), Review of Davis, L. and Proctor, E. in *Groupwork*, 3(1), 78–82, and correspondence in *Groupwork* 3(3), 302–303.

Ward, D. and Mullender, A. (1991), 'Facilitation in Self-directed Groupwork', *Groupwork*, 4(2).

Watson, D. (ed., 1985), *A Code of Ethics for Social Work* (London, Routledge and Kegan Paul).

Wayne, J. and Avery, N.C. (1980), *Child Abuse: Prevention and Treatment Through Social Groupwork* (Boston, Charles Rivers Books).

Weaver, C. and Fox, C. (1984), 'The Berkeley Sex Offenders Group: A Seven Year Evaluation', *Probation*, 31(4).

Werbin, J. and Hines, K. (1975), 'Transference and Culture in a Latino Therapy Group', *International Journal of Group Psychotherapy*, 25(4).

*Whitaker, D.S. (1976), 'Some Conditions for Effective Work with Groups', *British Journal of Social Work*, 5(4), 423–39.

*Whitaker, D.S. (1985), *Using Groups to Help People* (London, Routledge & Kegan Paul).

Whitaker, D. and Lieberman, M. (1964), *Psychotherapy Through the Group Process* (London, Tavistock).

Woodcock, M. (1979), *Team Development Manual* (Aldershot, Gower).

*Yalom, I.D. (1975, 1985 edns), *The Theory and Practice of Group Psychotherapy* (New York, Basic Books).

Ziller, R. (1965), 'Toward a Theory of Open and Closed Groups', *Psychological Bulletin*, LXIII.

Special issues of *Groupwork*:

Vol. 2(3), 1989, *Groupwork in Europe*
Vol. 3(2), 1990, *Child Sexual Abuse: The Groupwork Response*
Vol. 4(3), 1991, *Groupwork with Offenders*

Special issues of *Social Work with Groups* (=*SWG*):
Vol. 3(4), 1980, *Co-Leadership in Social Work with Groups*
Vol. 4(1), 1981, *Groupwork in Great Britain*
Vol. 5(1), 1982, *Social Groupwork and Alcoholism*
Vol. 5(2), 1982, *Groupwork with the Frail Elderly*
Vol. 5(4), 1982, *The Use of Group Services in Permanency Planning for Children*
Vol. 6(1), 1983, *Activities and Action in Groupwork*
Vol. 6(3/4), 1983, *Groupwork with Women/Groupwork with Men*
Vol. 7(3), 1984, *Ethnicity in Social Groupwork Practice*
Vol. 7(4), 1984, *Groupwork with Children and Adolescents*
Vol. 8(2), 1985, *Time as a Factor in Groupwork*
Vol. 8(4), 1985, *Legacy of William Schwartz*
Vol. 9(3), 1986, *Research in Social Groupwork*
Vol. 9(4), 1986, *Collectivity in Social Groupwork*
Vol. 10(2), 1987, *Working Effectively with Administrative Groups*
Vol. 11(1/2), 1988, *Groupwork Education/Training*
Vol. 11(3), 1988, *Violence: Prevention and Treatment in Groups*
Vol. 12(1), 1989, *Social Work with Multi-Family Groups*
Vol. 13(1), 1990, *Groupwork with the Emotionally Disabled*
Vol. 13(4), 1990, *Ethnicity and Biculturalism*
Vol. 14(1), 1991, *Groupwork with Suburbia's Children*

Author Index

Subject Index

anti-discrimination
guidelines for 154–8,
166–80
contract negotiation by
62–7, 74–5, 99, 103
decision making by 99–100
features of groupwork
affecting 17–18
gender of 49, 78, 82, 83,
164–5, 167–9, 174
group processes and 100–11
groups of 2, 138
planning of need for 44

problem solution by 123–30
race of 51, 78, 82, 83,
164–5, 167–9, 174
in residential care 133–4,
138, 140, 141–51
selection of 46, 60, 76–7
self-disclosure by 93–5,
133–4, 150–51
social class of 51–2
see also co-working;
leadership; training
writing in groups 115–16
written records 194–6